David Clarke has done it again! *Married...but Lonely* is an incredibly practical, biblical, and insightful book. Guys, read this book. You'll "rise up and call David Clarke blessed" when your wife "rises up and calls you blessed." And, oh yes, you'll thank me for recommending it to you.

—STEVE BROWN
PROFESSOR EMERITUS, REFORMED THEOLOGICAL SEMINARY
RADIO HOST, *KEY LIFE*
AUTHOR

It's time for intimacy in your marriage, isn't it? Do I have a book to recommend to you! Dr. David Clarke's *Married...but Lonely* has proven steps to get you and your spouse to the marriage you've always dreamed of having.

—PAT WILLIAMS
SENIOR VICE PRESIDENT, ORLANDO MAGIC
AUTHOR, *LEADERSHIP EXCELLENCE*

David Clarke has done it again! *Married...but Lonely* is a savvy mix of wit and wisdom, practical advice and biblical counsel that gets to the heart of the causes and cures of the intimacy-challenged husband. Both the clueless husband and the frustrated wife will find sensitive and thoughtful guidelines to discovering or rediscovering the intimacy every marriage deserves, every marriage requires.

—DR. WOODROW KROLL
PRESIDENT, BACK TO THE BIBLE

Dr. David Clarke's book *Married...but Lonely* addresses the issue of what women most want out of marriage and men are reluctant to give: intimacy! Understanding what men and women both need and want, Dr. Clarke gently leads couples into a deeper, lasting, and fulfilling relationship. For couples who know there is more "out there" than they have but didn't know what they were searching for, it's a must-read!

—HAROLD J. SALA, PhD
FOUNDER AND PRESIDENT,
GUIDELINES INTERNATIONAL MINISTRIES

MARRIED

BUT

LONELY

MARRIED
BUT
LONELY

DAVID E. CLARKE, PhD
with WILLIAM G. CLARKE, MA

SILOAM

Most CHARISMA HOUSE BOOK GROUP products are available at special quantity discounts for bulk purchase for sales promotions, premiums, fund-raising, and educational needs. For details, write Charisma House Book Group, 600 Rinehart Road, Lake Mary, Florida 32746, or telephone (407) 333-0600.

MARRIED...BUT LONELY
by David E. Clarke, PhD, with William G. Clarke
Published by Siloam
Charisma Media/Charisma House Book Group
600 Rinehart Road
Lake Mary, Florida 32746
www.charismahouse.com

Unless otherwise noted, all Scripture quotations are from the New American Standard Bible, copyright © 1960, 1962, 1963, 1968, 1971, 1972, 1973, 1975, 1977, 1995 by The Lockman Foundation. Used by permission. (www.Lockman.org)

Scripture quotations marked NIV are from the Holy Bible, New International Version. Copyright © 1973, 1978, 1984, International Bible Society. Used by permission.

Scripture quotations marked NLT are from the Holy Bible, New Living Translation, copyright © 1996, 2004, 2007. Used by permission of Tyndale House Publishers, Inc., Wheaton, IL 60189. All rights reserved.

Cover design by Lisa Cox
Design Director: Bill Johnson

Visit the author's website at www.davidclarkeseminars.com.

Library of Congress Cataloging-in-Publication Data:
Clarke, David, Ph. D.
  Married...but lonely / by David E. Clarke, PhD, with William G.
Clarke. -- First edition .
      pages cm
  Includes bibliographical references.
  ISBN 978-1-61638-698-6 (trade paper) -- ISBN 978-1-62136-005-6
(e-book)
  1. Marriage--Religious aspects--Christianity. 2. Man-woman
relations--Religious aspects--Christianity. I. Title.
  BV835.C5755 2013
  248.8'435--dc23
                                    2012046138

14 15 16 17 18 — 9 8 7 6 5
Printed in the United States of America

To Rocky Glisson

A loving husband to Debi

A great dad to Beth

A terrific therapist to his clients

And my best friend

Contents

Step Five
This Is Exactly the Kind of Wife I Need to Be

Step Six
I Need Your Help to Heal From My Past Pain

Step Seven
I Need to Get Tough and Rattle Your Cage

PART THREE
What if God Wants Me to Stay in a Lonely Marriage?

PART ONE
HELP! I CAN'T GET CLOSE TO MY HUSBAND

Chapter 1

He Automatically
Avoids Intimacy

To every woman reading this, regardless of income, social level, or educational background, the chances are very good that your husband has no idea of how *you* want him to get close to you. My research over the past two decades, as a clinical psychologist and as a speaker presenting marriage seminars nationwide, shows that 85 percent of all husbands have *no clue* when it comes to achieving closeness with their wives. However, to make absolutely sure, take my intimacy avoider (IA) Quiz:

He is content with low levels of intimacy in the marriage.	T	F
He does not talk in a personal, heart-to-heart way with you.	T	F
He holds his emotions and deep thoughts inside.	T	F
His idea of quality time is having you sit next to him while he watches TV.	T	F
He seems to love his TV, computer, and job more than he loves you.	T	F
He believes the only purpose of romance was to get you to marry him; after the wedding he dropped it.	T	F
The only time he is passionate is during sex.	T	F
He has the listening skills of a tree stump.	T	F

He's into conservation...of words. He sees no point in using twenty-five words when one or two will do.   T F

You have come to realize that 99 percent of his entire conversational repertoire with you consists of these twenty statements: T F

- "Fine."
- "OK."
- "Pretty good."
- "Sure."
- "I don't know."
- "Nothing's wrong."
- "I don't want to talk about it."
- "I said I was sorry."
- "Get over it."
- "You're overreacting."
- "You shouldn't feel that way."
- "I forgot."
- "I never said that."
- "It's that time of the month, isn't it?"
- "How about some sex, baby?"
- "What's on television?"
- "Do we have to visit your parents?"
- "Where are my socks?"
- "What's for dinner?"
- "What did you say?"

He would rather face a firing squad than talk through a conflict with you.   T F

He does love you but cannot express love in ways that make you feel loved.   T F

He is happy as long as you give him sex, food, clean clothes, and the remote control.	**T F**
He thinks you have a great marriage.	**T F**
He has no idea why you're upset and unhappy.	**T F**

If you answered true to at least ten of these statements, you are married to an IA. Because this is usually a male trait, throughout this book I refer to the husband as the intimacy avoider. For any husbands reading, those who are married to one of the 15 percent of female intimacy avoiders, these same principles apply. My strategy also applies to those in serious dating relationships and engaged couples. Before you get married, it's a good idea to make sure your partner can connect with you on a deeper level.

He Is Intimacy-Challenged

Your man isn't a bad guy. He is not mean or evil, hasn't killed anyone, and doesn't run over squirrels for sport. He is a moral, decent, and upright person who works hard at his job. He is not having an affair. He is not an alcoholic or a drug user, nor is he addicted to anything. He does not verbally or physically abuse you. He is solid, stable, and responsible. He is a good guy!

He even loves you. You know he loves you. The one problem with him—and it's a *big one*—is that he doesn't love you the way you need to be loved. He doesn't meet your deepest, most important need as a wife: to be emotionally connected to him. He doesn't open up and share himself with you. His feelings, personal thoughts, problems, worries, spiritual life, hopes, and dreams all stay buried inside. He is "intimacy-challenged."

The one area in which he seems to be able to give himself to you is sex. During foreplay or intercourse he can be warm, sensitive, and loving. But frankly that isn't good enough. You need him to give himself to you emotionally. Physical love without emotional connection is difficult—even painful—for you and does not meet your greatest need.

If this describes your marriage, you really and truly don't know your own husband. And you desperately want—actually need—to know him. That is why you married him: to be close to him! You need to know and experience who he really is inside. And you need him to know and experience who you really are inside. You may be thinking, "That hasn't happened in my marriage, and it doesn't look as though it's ever going to happen."

For true intimacy to happen, it takes two people—both spouses. This means he has to talk! He has to put aside his logic and let his emotions come out. He has to open up and share with you his personal stuff on a regular basis. As a woman you know this is true because you understand how intimacy works. But he just doesn't seem to get it, and he certainly isn't joining you in this intimacy process. You feel stuck at square one, because your man won't talk to you on a personal level.

Your man is emotionally stunted. He hides his true self behind an incredibly thick, seemingly impenetrable wall. He may even be a pretty expressive guy with a great sense of humor. I've known many men who have no trouble talking, but they close down when it comes to any personal, below-the-surface exchanges.

Oh, he will talk, but only about things that are safe and superficial: generalities about his day, facts, events, logical observations, financial matters, his schedule, home maintenance, the kids, or vacation plans... These are the kinds of things he could share with anyone: a friend; his dad, mom, or brother; or the mail carrier. But you're his *wife*! You need more than this!

Anything but Closeness

Your husband is a master at avoiding intimacy. He has been doing it his whole life. Like the Great Houdini, he is a world-class escape artist. He will do whatever it takes to weasel out of a close, deep conversation. Do any of these favorite escape-from-closeness tricks sound familiar?

Answering a question with a question

You ask him, "How are you doing?" He responds, "Why do you ask?" You're thinking, "What do you mean, 'why do I ask?' I'm trying to start a conversation. I want to get to know you better." So you ask, "What are you thinking?" and he responds with a question that makes no sense: "Who knows?" Meanwhile, you're thinking, "Duh! The only person who knows would be you!"

Pleading ignorance

One of the classic male IA escape lines to any question requiring personal information is, "I don't know." That is a beautiful, inoffensive way to kill conversations. What he's really telling you is, "I'd love to talk to you, honey, but I have no information. If only I could think of one thing that happened to me today, but I can't. Sorry. My mind's a complete blank." It's amazing how men know zilch when you are trying to get a conversation going. The fact is, he just doesn't want to talk and this "brain cramp" is a wonderful excuse.

Massive generalizations

You ask, "How was your day?" and he answers, "Fine" or "OK." Too bad you can't build much of a conversation on these two global replies. Of course that is why he responds this way. He doesn't want to give you anything to work with. He has courteously answered your question and escaped any possibility of closeness. It's as if you asked, "Where do you live?" and he responded, "In the Milky Way Galaxy."

No response

He simply does not respond to your questions. Like the Great Sphinx of Egypt, his face and body are carved out of stone. You could stick him with a pin—admit it, that is tempting—and he wouldn't react. You're thinking, "Am I here? Do I exist? Is he in some parallel universe? Did he hear me?" Oh, he heard you all right. He is exercising elective mutism. He is letting you know that he doesn't want to talk about whatever topic you have brought up.

Refusal to talk

How many times has your husband told you, "I don't want to talk about it" and its time-honored corollary, "This isn't a good time to talk"? He is tired, stressed, too full from dinner, the ball game is coming on, or he has a crick in his neck. He seems to indicate that sometime, someday, somewhere, there will be a good time to talk. Believe me, you won't live long enough to reach that time.

Letting you talk all the time

While he is usually happy to let you talk, he doesn't listen too closely. After all, if you fill the air with words, he doesn't have to talk. There is no intimacy in a monologue. Intimacy requires a dialogue, so he avoids it by encouraging you to ramble on alone.

Snap then leave

He'll get angry, snap some nasty comment at you, and leave the room. Since standing up and stalking out would be too obvious, he cleverly creates a ruse to escape your conversational clutches. If you get angry or exasperated—which is perfectly understandable—that plays right into his hands. He'll say you're overreacting, which gives him an excuse to leave. He doesn't *really want to leave* (yeah, right), but you made him angry and so he has to split.

Drop it and move on

When you try to talk through a conflict, he will accuse you of dwelling on the past. He fails to recognize that the past is not the past until you have dealt with it together and reached a mutual understanding. He may use statements such as, "I said I was sorry," or, "Stop bringing that up" to end the conflict. He believes that if you drop the subject, the problem will magically vanish.

Too busy to talk

He is a busy, busy man with many important things to do; sadly, that just doesn't leave any time to talk with you. He has to work, watch television, dink around on the computer, do yard work, fix things around the house, read the paper, sleep, or whatever else he can find to avoid conversation with you.

Can't talk but can have sex

Ever try to talk and your spouse starts fondling you? You're trying to connect emotionally, and your conversationally impaired husband is in groping mode! Why waste time talking when you can have sex? When you don't respond favorably (what a shocker), he gets offended and accuses you of rejecting him. Now, because you have made him angry and pouty, he certainly can't be expected to talk to you.

The logical man

Since he buries his emotions, he is aware only of cold, hard logic. When you get emotional, he doesn't see it as a normal, healthy female reaction. He sees it as a bizarre, unnecessary, and frightening monster that must be stamped out immediately. He tries his logic to talk you out of your feelings: "Honey, you shouldn't feel that way." "Honey, you're way too intense." "Honey, calm down and let's look at the facts." "Honey, listen up, and I'll tell you how to fix your problem." Of course, his logic both infuriates and hurts you. Conversation over.

The martyr

When you press him to talk, he'll say in a whiny, pitiful voice, "I guess I can't ever please you." It is almost amusing how his refusal to talk becomes your fault because you can't be pleased. Your expectations are too high. You want too much. This poor, dear man has tried his little heart out and it is not good enough for you. This clever ruse is nothing more than a distraction from the real issue. Your expectation of him talking and sharing himself is reasonable. You want what every wife wants!

The genetic excuse

If all else fails, your IA will resort to these old standards:

- "Hey, this is who I am."

- "You knew I was like this when you married me."

- "I can't change."

Bogus. Bogus. Bogus. It may be who he is, but he doesn't have to stay that way. Unless you were freeze-dried right after the wedding and put into cold storage, you both need to change as the marriage progresses. He can change, and he needs to if you're going to build an intimate relationship. I tell husbands who use the genetic excuse, "I guess if you had a huge, painful boil the size of a basketball on your neck, you would just keep it there. After all, it's who you are. Baloney! You get rid of something if it's causing real damage. Your being an intimacy avoider is causing real damage to your marriage."

Sound familiar? I'll bet it does. What your husband fails to realize is that all his intimacy-avoidance techniques are hurting him, you, and your marriage. He isn't intentionally causing damage and pain. Sidestepping closeness is automatic for him. It comes naturally. He has no idea he is keeping himself and you from an intimate, joyful life together.

Why Did You Marry an Intimacy Avoider?

There are three possible reasons:

1. You had no clue; you were "in love."

You had no clue he was into intimacy avoiding. You were "in love" with him. Head-over-heels crazy about him. Totally infatuated. He was the greatest guy in the world: drop-dead handsome, witty, expressive, kind, charming, and able to meet all of your needs. You couldn't believe how lucky you were to find such a perfect man.

By definition your infatuated brain blinded you to the reality that you were dating a man who didn't understand true closeness. Infatuation put a wonderful glow around him and made whatever he said seem deep and personal and revealing:

- "I like that dress."

- "I had a lousy day at work."

- "I think there's a rock in my shoe."

- "Bugs Bunny is my favorite cartoon character."

These statements were fascinating, stimulating, and devastatingly insightful to you. No! No, they weren't! They were superficial! But you didn't know that. By the time the truth dawned on you, it was too late. You were married.

2. You may have realized he had IA traits before you married him, but in your love-crazed mind, you were convinced you could change him.

Your thinking went something like: "When we're married, we will be closer. It will all work out. He will open up when he knows me better. Being with me more will really help. He isn't so bad at communicating. He is really sensitive and has real depth.

He just needs to feel loved and safe. Then he will talk to me on a personal level."

Wrong on all counts! As you found out later, marriage did not bring you closer; it made things worse. Faced with being with you 24/7, he put his IA techniques into hyperdrive to keep himself safe from your constant attempts to "get close." He knew you better because you talked and shared yourself. He figured that was fine for you to do. That was your choice. But it didn't motivate him to reveal himself. Turns out, he is a terrible communicator—about as sensitive as a block of wood. He isn't deep. He's superficial. All the love in the world won't open him up. He is a man, and a man's primary purpose in relationships is to avoid opening up.

The truth is, you can help him change, but not the way you've been going about it.

3. You didn't have much of a chance to dodge the bullet.
The vast majority of men on Earth fall into this category.

Being Married to an
Intimacy Avoider Isn't Pretty

Well, you married him, and now you're stuck. He just won't talk personally, will he? You have tried everything. You've been nice and loving. It doesn't work. You've cried and begged. It doesn't work. You have prayed your heart out, been angry and demanding, and given him the silent treatment. Even threatened him. It doesn't work. It doesn't work. It doesn't work!

You have dragged him to church and to marriage seminars. You've tried to get him to read marriage books, but most men don't read. If he does read, he doesn't apply what he reads to himself. You've bought audiotapes and videotapes, amassing one of the largest private collections of marriage material in the civilized world. Nothing has worked. *Nothing.*

At best your marriage is OK. On good days it might even

reach the level of "pretty good." However, it is more likely that your marriage is dying or already dead. Without an ongoing emotional connection—and if you are reading this, chances are you don't have one—there can be no real life in a marriage.

He is not meeting your emotional needs. You don't feel understood by him. You don't feel nurtured or cherished. You feel disconnected from him. You are angry, resentful, and deeply hurt. This is not the marriage you dreamed of having. It's not even close.

The Way to Change

Admit it. You are weary and losing hope. You tell yourself it could be worse. You are right—it could be. He is a decent guy. He is not abusive. He loves you, and you still love him. But you aren't willing to settle for the mediocre, superficial bonds you have now. You know what you're missing. You dread living out your life in this, "OK, so we have no closeness, no-real-passion, just-get-along marriage."

Guess what? You don't have to settle. There is a way to change. You can do something about it. You don't have to stay stuck. You can help your husband become a man who talks, shares himself, and meets your need for emotional intimacy. You can turn your marriage into the close, intimate, loving relationship you've always wanted and need. My strategy has helped thousands of wives transform their marriages. It has worked for them, and it will work for you. Turn the page and let's get to work.

Chapter 2

=====

Yes, He Can Change

THERE ARE TWO myths in the Christian community—and popular culture—that can prevent wives from developing intimate marriages. Well-meaning authors, radio personalities, clueless celebrities, church members, and even pastors keep these myths alive. If you believe either, you are doomed to always have a husband who is unable to meet the important needs God built into women.

MYTH #1:
Just Keep on Loving Him, and He'll Change

This myth proclaims that if you keep on faithfully loving him and meeting his needs, he will eventually respond by meeting your needs. Supposedly you don't have to say a word (though you may have already said too many); just focus on being positive and cheerful while doing everything you can to make him happy. Unable to resist your steady outpouring of love, he will spend the rest of his life making you feel cherished and close to him.

This approach is a complete misunderstanding of a man's nature. He doesn't even realize he isn't meeting your needs. Unless you tell him, he will literally never know. If he sees you acting content, he will assume you are content. Because you continue doing all the usual things for him, he remains convinced that you are happy and everything in your marriage is fine. It never dawns on him that you are dying a slow death from lack of intimacy—the kind you knew and loved when you were dating.

By the way, how is the "change him with love and kindness" approach working? You've been at it now for a number of years. Yeah, I thought so. Not changing, is he? You may be wondering if there is any truth to the words of 1 Peter 3:1–2: "In the same way, you wives, be submissive to your own husbands so that even if any of them are disobedient to the word, they may be won without a word by the behavior of their wives, as they observe your chaste and respectful behavior."

These verses teach submission, *not* subservience or passivity. Although a wife is always to model purity and excellent behavior, she is also to follow the verses that instruct her to speak up in a loving, firm way. The Proverbs 31 wife, a wonderful model for all wives, was very assertive and active, and her husband respected her. He "trusts in her" (v. 11). Other passages teach that we should confront sin (Matt. 18:15–17) and speak the truth (Eph. 4:15; Col. 3:9). The bottom line: When you look at the whole of Scripture, you see God instructing wives to model submission and excellent behavior *and* to be assertive and worthy of respect.

MYTH #2:
He's Doing the Best He Can

This second myth tells you that your man isn't that bad and that you will be OK if he doesn't change. Right now you may be trying to reassure yourself, "He's a good man. He works hard at his job. He goes to church. He doesn't beat me, drink like a fish, or sleep around. He could be a lot worse. I have to accept the fact that he won't change. I can live with that."

You have given up hope of having a deeper, more intimate bond with your man. His lack of openness and communication does hurt you, but you think they can't be helped. So you paint on your brave smile and keep walking on that long, lonely road toward the horizon.

Some older wives in your church family or social circle may have convinced you that the man you have is as good as he can get. They have persuaded you that men are "just that way," and you can do nothing about it. For good measure they may have thrown in the classic enabler line: "Honey, you just have to make Jesus your husband."

These two myths are wrong. Wrong. Wrong. Wrong. You are sadly mistaken if you believe your husband will change because of your excellent behavior. You are also in error if you believe your husband can't change and is incapable of meeting your needs. In either case *you* are part of the problem. You are enabling him to remain exactly the kind of husband he is now. Since he is convinced that you are OK with the way he is, he feels zero motivation to do anything differently.

If you have bought into one of these two myths, it is time to wake up, smell the coffee, and see the truth. It's time for another approach—one that has a very good chance of turning your man into a great husband who knows how to be truly intimate with you.

An Ephesians 5:25 Husband

God makes it very clear what kind of husband He wants your husband to be:

> Husbands, love your wives, just as Christ also loved the church and gave Himself up for her.
> —EPHESIANS 5:25

How did Christ love the church? How does Christ continue to love the church? With gentleness, care, nurturing, and selfless service. By listening, connecting, and meeting every important need. IA husbands don't love this way. Indeed they cannot because in their present state they are not able to open up, talk, understand, and communicate beyond a surface level.

God Will Use You to
Help Your Husband Change

God may have created your husband with a rather stoic nature, but He doesn't want him to remain this way. God wants him to become an Ephesians 5:25 husband, but your husband doesn't even know he has a problem with intimacy! How in the world is he going to become a sensitive, loving, and Christlike spouse? There is only one way. I am convinced God wants to use *you* to help your husband change. That is why He brought you together.

Working with wives to influence their husbands is a huge part of what I do in my clinical psychology practice. One of my specialties is guiding them through the process of helping their spouses become godly men who can express their personal thoughts and feelings, communicate on deeper levels, and meet needs. Even if their husbands never darken the door of my therapy office, never read one of my books, and never attend one of my marriage seminars, these wives—with God's help and power—can create amazing changes in their husbands. So can you.

To begin the process of "IA Husband Transformation," you need two things.

- To understand what makes a man intimacy-challenged
- A proven strategy to change him into the husband you need him to be, and for you to be changed into the wife that he needs you to be

He Was Born That Way

Your husband was intimacy-challenged from the point of conception, during the nine months he spent inside momma, and when he took his first breath and screamed because someone slapped his little intimacy-challenged bottom. God used testosterone and creative brain wiring to gear his entire personality toward action not communication. By nature, men are doers, not talkers. Women are born talkers and would rather talk than do anything else. My wife, Sandy, and I have observed this dramatic difference between the sexes among our four children. Emily, Leeann, and Nancy came first. Finally God gave us William. The girls love to talk. They live to talk. There aren't enough hours in the day to handle all their words. Leeann and Nancy even talk in their sleep!

My girls talk with us and with each other. They talk on the phone with their friends. They talk on the computer in long, expressive e-mails and via Facebook. At home I haven't spoken on the phone or used my computer for two years. I can't get on either one! Their supply of conversational information is endless. My Emily will spend three hours with some friends at a party, talking the whole time. When she gets home, she'll immediately go to the computer so she can talk with these same friends about what they just talked about for three hours at the party!

My girls jump from topic to topic. Every topic, no matter how trivial, is important because it can lead to a whole chain reaction of interesting conversational tidbits. Here is a recent conversation—I should say monologue—I had with Leeann:

> Dad, that's a nice shirt you have on. Is that a light green stripe? My girlfriend Bobbi was wearing a skirt two weeks ago with a light green stripe. She got in trouble with her mom because her skirt was too short. They had a bad argument out by their pool. The pool was dirty, so her mom blamed her for that too. Her little dog, Fluffy, a white and brown wiener dog who has kidney problems, came running up just then and tried to jump into her arms. Bobbi didn't

see her coming, so she jerked back in surprise, and Fluffy jumped right into the pool. It was hilarious!

You know, I saw another dog last Thursday that looked like Fluffy. By the way, did I mention that I saw Fluffy once? Bobbi brought her to school one morning. That was the same morning I broke my favorite yellow hairbrush. I loved that hairbrush. Anyway, this other dog was wearing a cute little red and black checked vest. My friend Ashley had bought that same kind of vest last March when we were shopping at the mall. Can you believe that? I remember that the salesperson had bright purple hair, a nose ring, and a bad attitude. She was rude to Ashley and me. Oh, there were so many weird things that happened that day at the mall! We were just getting dropped off at the entrance by her mom when…

This was just the first two and a half minutes of the conversation. Leeann was just warming up! I don't have room to put on paper the other twenty minutes. Can you see how important it was to notice the light green stripe? Women talk the way paleontologists create prehistoric animal models for museums. From one chipped tooth these scientists build an entire dinosaur. Women can construct an entire conversation from one tiny, inconsequential fact. Amazing!

And then God created William. And then there was destruction. And then there was yelling, running, climbing, wild laughter, and loud animal noises. And constant activity. Like almost all boys—and men—seven-year-old William is a doer. From the moment he wakes up at the crack of dawn (he slept in an extra hour exactly two days in his first seven years) to the moment he finally goes to sleep at night, William is doing something. He plays video games, computer games, rides his bike, swims in the pool, engages in every outdoor sport known to mankind with his buddies, plays board games and card games, and bugs his sisters.

If he watches television or a movie, it had better be sports-oriented or filled with nonstop, dramatic action.

William talks, but only about four things: what he has done, what he is doing right now, what he is going to do, and sports. If he's not doing something, he is miserable. He can't stand sitting around and talking. He hates chick movies. He is not sensitive. Understanding his sisters and their feelings isn't even on his radar screen. He just wants to play, play, play, and do, do, do.

Like nearly all women, girls talk because they have a God-given need to connect with others and develop closeness in their relationships. Like most men, William is a doer because he has a God-given need to compete with others and maintain control in relationships. If William is going to be a good husband some day, he will have to learn to open up and communicate with a woman. While Sandy and I are trying to teach him these skills, it is an uphill battle. It goes against his nature. He just doesn't get it...yet.

He Was Raised That Way

IA men aren't just born. They are also made. Chances are your husband's parents raised him to be this way. Now, they didn't sit down and plan it this way: "We want little Timmy to become a good, solid, intimacy-challenged husband, so here is what we each have to do to make sure that happens." Yet Mom and Dad still got the job done. He's intimacy-challenged, isn't he?

Take a close look at your husband's father. I bet you will see an intimacy-challenged man—your husband's original role model. Just as a master craftsman teaches his apprentice, your father-in-law taught your husband the proud, honorable trade of avoiding intimacy. Through years of modeling he trained his son to carry on the family pattern. He passed the anti-intimacy torch to the next generation.

Your husband probably never—and I mean that literally—saw

a significant man in his life share something personal. It just didn't happen. Dad didn't do it. Nor did his grandfathers. Not his brother, nor Uncle Harry, nor any of his male teachers or coaches. So he learned not to share personal things with other men, and certainly not with women.

What he did observe, repeatedly for many years, was Dad and other key men in his life choke back emotions, stuff personal reactions, refuse to answer personal questions posed by women, say as little as possible and stick to the facts, be logical, avoid conflicts, and show emotion only when watching sports.

Chances are your husband also saw his mom and dad develop and maintain a marriage devoid of real intimacy. It was a marriage of an IA and an IA Enabler. He saw his mom carry on bravely for years, enabling her intimacy-avoiding husband and acting as if everything was OK. The truth was she felt unhappy and terribly unfulfilled, just as you feel now. However, your husband couldn't discern his mother's pain. He thought—and still does—that his parents' marriage was "fine." He actually believes the relationship they had (and still may have) is as good as it gets. He will say things such as:

- "They had a good marriage."
- "They got along."
- "They never fought."
- "They built a solid, stable life together."

Wonderful. Doesn't sound too exciting and passionate, does it? Yet if his parents got divorced or had obvious trouble in their marriage, he would probably have no idea why. Is it any wonder he does not know how to be intimate with you? All the men he grew up around modeled IA behavior. As a result, he never saw a man and a woman engage in a personal, deep conversation. He's never experienced emotional intimacy with another person. He has no idea what it takes to get it or how to achieve it. All he knows is how to avoid intimacy. He has those skills down cold. After all, he was trained by the best.

Shaped By Culture

As if all this wasn't enough—and believe me, it is—American culture finishes the job of making your man resist intimacy in relationships. Read this brief list of movie stars and picture the kind of men they have portrayed on screen:

- John Wayne
- Sylvester Stallone
- Humphrey Bogart
- Harrison Ford
- Robert Mitchum
- Arnold Schwarzenegger
- Clint Eastwood
- Bruce Willis

It's an easy exercise, isn't it? These stars have played open, sensitive, romantic, gentle, and caring men. Men who share their feelings openly, without shame or defensiveness. Men who have made it their primary goal in life to tenderly meet the needs of the women in their lives. Yeah, right!

All these actors have played hard-edged, macho, tough-as-steel, independent, and emotionally distant men. The only emotion they've displayed is anger at their on-screen enemies. They don't talk much and don't bother with romance. They keep personal thoughts and feelings to themselves. Through the power of film these "movie star IAs" have taught generations of men that remaining in control and emotionless is what manhood is all about. It may work in the movies, but it *doesn't* work in marriage.

Movies aren't the only medium that helps shape a man's view of self. American culture pushes men to avoid intimacy by placing a massive emphasis on career success. If you're not making serious money in a high-profile, impressive job in America, you're a loser. A hapless, pitiful loser. Newspapers, magazines, Internet sites, and TV news shows profile corporate CEOs and entrepreneurs who have amassed power, fame, and fortune. Most of these men are workaholics who have gone through two or three wives and left damaged children in their wake. But who cares? They're rich! They've made it! They're real men!

Most men feel insecure because of this unrelenting cultural pressure to succeed in their careers and provide for their families. Unlike women, who can define themselves as wives and mothers, men have only careers to define them. With few relationship skills, men are unable to get their needs met from wives, children, or friends. By default they are forced to focus on their jobs in order to feel some sense of accomplishment and success.

Men cover their insecurities by putting up a tough, confident exterior. They talk only about superficial subjects in which they feel competent: work, the stock market, sports, cars, things that need fixing, current events, politics, or the weather. Even when men talk to other men, few say anything deep or personal. They stick with what they know and feel safe talking about. They stay in control and unconnected to others.

Escape From Relationship Prison

Well, you have your work cut out for you. As you can see, there are powerful forces that created and continue to keep your husband a person who shuns closeness in relationships. In a very real sense your husband is imprisoned behind huge walls that shut his inner life off from the outside world—specifically from you.

His prison has bigger walls and better security than the infamous Alcatraz Island in San Francisco Bay.

Your mission, should you choose to accept it, is to help your man break out of his prison and join you in the land of emotion, expression, and communication. Remember, he doesn't even realize he is locked up! But he is, and breaking out will be good for him, you, and your children. Once he gets a taste of intimacy, he is going to want it. You have to give him that taste.

A "Mission Impossible" Strategy

How can you pull off this seemingly impossible mission? With God's help and the right strategy. Here's a brief overview of my seven-step Husband Transformation Strategy:

Step one: "I need a team."

You need a team alongside to help your husband change. A team will provide strength, accountability, and endurance. With God, your church, and a few close friends, you have the foundation in place to launch the mission.

Step two: "This is exactly the kind of husband I need you to be."

Chances are close to 100 percent that your husband has no idea of your real needs. It is time to tell him exactly what you have needed over the years—and still need—from him. But it won't be only the needs *you* think you have. It will be the needs *God* says your husband is to meet.

Step three: "Honey, I need to forgive you."

In order to team up with your husband in this change process, you must release all the pent-up bitterness and hurt clogging your insides. On paper you will vent—in complete detail—the resentments you have harbored against him from the day you met to the day you write this letter. You will also forgive him for everything, intentional and unintentional, he has said or done to harm you. Without asking for or expecting a response, you will regularly tell him (honestly and directly) your needs and reactions to his treatment of you. This will model expression of emotions and keep your emotional system clean and your needs ever before him.

Step four: "I need to know how I am killing our intimacy."

It is very likely you are acting in ways that prevent your husband from opening up. Unwittingly you could be helping your husband stay locked up, which is the last thing you want to do. You need to discover these mistakes and stop making them.

Step five: "This is exactly the kind of wife I need to be."

God has communicated a specific set of instructions in the Bible for wives. He knows what your husband needs from you, so listen to Him. First, God says be submissive. I will cover what submission does and doesn't mean. Second, God says be worthy of respect. Third, God says initiate affection and sex.

Step six: "I need your help to heal from my past pain."

Your unresolved pain from the past affects you in the present. It transfers to your marital relationship and limits the intimacy you can achieve. As you work through your pain and include your husband in the process, two things happen: 1) you heal and automatically become a better wife, and 2) your husband can finally connect with you on a deeper level and get in touch with his own emotions.

Step seven: "I need to get tough and rattle your cage."

If steps one through six don't change your husband, you have an industrial strength IA on your hands. You're going to have to bring out the big, biblical guns. Your husband is sinning, and he must now face consequences and confrontation.

Yes, your good man can become a great husband. How? By the two of you relying on God and carrying out these seven steps. Do these steps in order. Don't skip any.

Many wives have followed this strategy and seen tremendous results. Now it is your turn. By the time you finish working through the seven steps, there is a good chance there will be one less intimacy-challenged man in the world and one more great marriage.

PART TWO
SEVEN STEPS
TO A NEW HUSBAND

STEP ONE
I NEED A TEAM

Chapter 3

Your Mission Impossible Team

I LOVE THE *MISSION Impossible* movies. Based on the great old TV show that aired from 1966–1973, these movies are a nonstop thrill ride. Exciting, hair-raising action. Bad guys get killed, left and right. In each one there's a diabolically evil madman, amazing stunts, and the world is saved from annihilation—all to that incredibly cool theme music. Ah, great guy movies...

Tom Cruise plays Ethan Hunt, the unflappable leader of an elite, highly trained, super-secret team of American agents. Ethan and his small, hand-picked team receive assignments that are unbelievably difficult, extremely dangerous, and...well, impossible. As you likely know, Ethan is given his assignment via audiotape. After he listens to the jaw-dropping, spine-tingling description of the mission, the tape self-destructs in a poof of smoke. Right before it does, the voice says, "Your mission, should you choose to accept it..."

I have a fantasy that one time Ethan says, "Accept this mission? What, are you crazy? Forget it! I don't want to die. Get some other sucker to do it." Of course, he never does. He is too cool and gutsy. Ethan always says yes, gathers his team of agents, and goes to work.

How do they pull off these impossible missions? Two reasons: 1) these are movies with successful outcomes written into the scripts, and 2) Ethan and his agents are a *team*. They achieve their goals only by relying on and supporting each other. They work together. Alone, they would be helpless and not stand a chance. Together, they are strong and effective.

Women, you too have what may seem like an impossible mission: to change your husband. It can be done, but not by yourself. Just like Ethan Hunt, you need a team. Let me introduce you to them.

Got God?

God is the most important member of your mission impossible team. Other team members may come and go or sometimes let you down. Not God. He will always be with you to give you strength, patience, endurance, and whatever other help you may need. I'm not saying this because it sounds good and I *hope* it's true. This is what the Bible says:

> "I WILL NEVER DESERT YOU, NOR WILL I EVER FORSAKE YOU," so that we confidently say, "THE LORD IS MY HELPER, I WILL NOT BE AFRAID. WHAT WILL MAN DO TO ME?"
> —HEBREWS 13:5–6

Who gave Sarah, Abraham's wife, a child when she was over ninety years old (Gen. 21)? Who protected Jochebed's infant son, Moses, and allowed her to raise him in his early years (Exod. 2)? Who spared Rahab and her family when all the other inhabitants of Jericho perished (Josh. 6)? Who gave Deborah the victory over Israel's Canaanite oppressors (Judg. 4–5)? Who brought Ruth from a vulnerable, desperate situation to a life of joy and security with her new husband, Boaz (Book of Ruth)? Who released Abigail from her rotten, foolish husband, Nabal, and blessed her with her marriage to David (1 Sam. 25)? Who gave Esther the courage to risk her life and used her to save the Jews from destruction (Book of Esther)? Who raised a widow's son from the dead (Luke 7)? Who helped a hemorrhaging woman (Luke 8)? A crippled woman (Luke 13)? God! God did all these things.

All the women I just listed were trapped in hopeless situations, and God delivered them. He gave them exactly what they needed. God loves the impossible. Luke 1:37 says, "For nothing will be impossible with God." God does His best work when situations seem impossible. If God can help these women, He can help you.

To have God on your team, you need to be close to Him. You need to build your faith. You need to be a godly woman. God always rewards a faithful, godly woman. Always. Here's a great description of a godly woman:

> Your adornment must not be merely external—braiding the hair, and wearing gold jewelry, or putting on dresses; but let it be the hidden person of the heart, with the imperishable quality of a gentle and quiet spirit, which is precious in the sight of God.
>
> —1 PETER 3:3–4

God is not interested in what you look like on the outside. He is interested in what you are like on the inside. Your spiritual life, your connection and relationship to Him—that is what is precious in His sight. That is what He wants you to develop and nurture. And in return, God will give you many benefits. Here are four benefits that specifically apply to the wife of an intimacy avoider:

True beauty

Physical beauty fades. No matter how attractive you may be today, you won't stay that way forever. Everybody gets old. The wrinkles, gray hair, and other indignities of age creep closer with each passing year. And there's nothing you can do about it. Spiritual beauty, however, improves with age. The most beautiful women I know are in their sixties, seventies, and eighties.

31

They are godly, spiritual women who love Jesus. The inner light of Christ radiates from them. That is beauty!

The power to be a good wife

It is not difficult to live with a man. It is impossible! How can you love a man:

- Who watches ESPN, *Wall Street Week*, the Weather Channel, or some inane sitcom on television instead of talking honestly with you?

- Who expects the Medal of Honor for completing one three-minute household job?

- Whose only comment after you both have finished watching an beautiful, incredibly romantic, heartbreaking movie is: "My popcorn tasted a little stale"?

- Who thinks he's being Mr. Romantic when he rolls you over at 2:00 a.m. for five minutes of passionate, meaningful sex?

The answer is, *you can't*! If you try to love your IA in human strength alone, you may end up mumbling to yourself in a rubber room at the psychiatric ward. Or become a bitter, frustrated woman. But with God's help you can love him. With His power you can continue to love your husband and be a good wife to him. As you grow spiritually and stay close to God, you will live out the prayer expressed in Ephesians 3:16: "That He would grant you, according to the riches of His glory, to be strengthened with power through His Spirit in the inner man."

Your most important needs will be met

The fact is your IA is not meeting some of your most important and personal needs as a wife, such as emotional connection, feeling loved and cherished, true companionship, a spiritual bond, and romance. Even if your IA is doing the best that an IA can do, it isn't nearly enough to fill up your need tank. That hurts. Every day.

Because these needs are so important, it is easy to make it your number-one goal in life to get your spouse to meet them. When your efforts fail, you can become even more hurt and devastated. You begin to believe that your husband is ruining your life: "He's keeping me from being happy and fulfilled. He's wasting the best years of my life. He's making me miserable."

Actually he isn't. You're doing that to yourself because you have placed your husband at the top of your priority list. You have become obsessed with all the things he is *not doing* for you and all the needs he is *not meeting*. Your husband is not meeting some of your most important needs. That's true. It ought to be a goal of yours to change that situation. That's also true. That's why you are reading this book. However, *you cannot afford to make your husband and his poor relationship skills the main focus of your life.*

Only one Person belongs on the top of your priority list. Only one Person can meet your needs while your IA is still an IA. You know who that Person is: God. When you put God first and work on continually growing closer to Him, He will keep you from obsessing about your husband. He will love you, comfort you, and give you *His* joy and security. He will provide you with powerful spiritual and emotional strength. He will help you be the best wife under the circumstances that any intimacy avoider ever had.

Take hope in the Word of God, as expressed by the apostle Paul:

> In any and every circumstance I have learned the secret of being filled and going hungry, both at having abundance and suffering need. I can do all things through Him who strengthens me.
> —Philippians 4:12–13

Jesus Himself promises to meet your needs in the midst of difficult and painful circumstances:

> Come to Me, all who are weary and heavy-laden, and I will give you rest. Take My yoke upon you, and learn from Me, for I am gentle and humble in heart; and YOU WILL FIND REST FOR YOUR SOULS.
> —MATTHEW 11:28–29

When your husband does not meet your needs day after day and month after month, it still hurts. You still suffer, even if you stay close to God. But God will sustain you until your husband changes. If your husband does not change, God will be there for you. God will meet your most important needs. That is His promise to you.

You will know the best way to change your man spiritually

Every Christian wife I have spoken to—every one—has told me one of her heartfelt desires is for her husband to be a godly man who walks with Jesus and leads her spiritually. Yet precious few wives have a husband like that. One of the best ways to influence a man spiritually is to model a Christian life that works. Peter wrote these words to Christian wives whose husbands were not living godly lives:

> So that even if any of them are disobedient to the word, they may be won without a word by the behavior of their wives, as they observe your chaste and respectful behavior.
> —1 PETER 3:1–2

By showing him daily your close, loving relationship with God, it can make a major impact on his spirituality. It is his responsibility to grow spiritually—to change in any way, really—but you can help. You can make all the difference.

I have been married to my beautiful blonde Sandy for more than twenty-nine years. For all those years and more her commitment to Christ has helped me grow spiritually. Her impact on my spiritual life began as soon as we met at Point Loma College in San Diego, California.

I was the mature, confident sophomore, and Sandy the shy, star-struck freshman. OK, I was the awkward, bumbling sophomore who couldn't believe this gorgeous freshman was interested in him! Immediately Sandy's spirituality impressed me. One of the first places she invited me was to a Bible study in her dorm. I went (of course, I would have gone with her to a tractor pull). Seeing her love for Jesus motivated me to work on my relationship with Jesus. That is still true today.

Come to Christ

You can't be close to God unless you know Him. And you can't know Him unless you know His Son, Jesus Christ. He is essential to faith, the only way to know the Father, and the only way to eternal life. Jesus said:

> I am the way, and the truth, and the life; no one comes to the Father, but through Me.
> —JOHN 14:6

> This is eternal life, that they may know You, the only true God, and Jesus Christ whom You have sent.
> —JOHN 17:3

If you haven't already made that decision, here is what you must believe to become a Christian and establish a relationship with the one true God:

> For I delivered to you as of first importance what I also received, that Christ died for our sins according to the Scriptures, and that He was buried, and that He was raised on the third day according to the Scriptures.
> —1 CORINTHIANS 15:3–4

God loves you so much that He sent His only Son, Jesus, to die for all your sins. Jesus died a horrible death on the cross so that your sins would no longer separate you from God. Then, to prove He is God and has the power to forgive your sins, Jesus rose from the dead. When you believe these truths about Christ, you will establish a permanent, saving relationship with God.

Grow in Christ

Once you know Christ, it is critically important for you to *grow* in your relationship with Him. As you get closer to Jesus, you will also get closer to God the Father and God the Holy Spirit. All three members of the Godhead are vital to your spiritual health.

Spend individual time with Jesus every day. Use this time to talk to Him in prayer. Listen to His responses. Read and meditate on Bible passages and apply what you read and study to your daily life. Pray throughout the day, keeping in close contact with Jesus as you face the challenges and people He brings your way. Be part of a local church too. Listen to the Bible being taught. Build relationships with other Christians. Serve others in the church, using the gifts and talents God has given you.

If you have a husband who is not spiritually attuned to God, do not let that prevent you from growing spiritually. If he tells you not to go to church, inform him you intend to obey God and go anyway. If you have kids, take them with you. If he says you can attend church but not get involved in Sunday school or any area of service, inform him that you can't grow spiritually and obey God by just attending. Hear him out politely, then get as involved in your church as God wants you to be.

Invite your husband to pray with you. If he refuses, continue to pray and build your relationship with God. Invite him to join you in family devotions. If he refuses, you lead the children in a weekly time of Bible reading and prayer.

One Best Friend

Have you ever seen *Anne of Green Gables*? It's an excellent PBS series based on the best-selling novel by Canadian author Lucy Maud Montgomery about the adventures of a feisty orphan girl who is adopted by a brother and sister in their sixties. The scenery of Prince Edward Island is spectacular, the acting superb, and the story terrific. Don't tell my male buddies, but I love this series.

One of the most endearing parts of the series is the relationship between the orphan girl, Anne Shirley, and her best friend, Diana Berry. Scared and lonely as she arrives on the island, Anne finds strength, security, and love through her friendship with Diana. They talk together, laugh together, and cry together. They share their lives—triumphs, trials, and experiences—as only two women can. Anne calls Diana her bosom friend and kindred spirit.

I believe that every woman (and every man) needs a best friend. Like Anne Shirley, a woman needs another woman to be her kindred spirit. God is your number-one team member, but your kindred spirit is number two. Living with an IA and working to change him is difficult; you need a buddy to stand with you to support you, listen to you vent your pain and heartache, and give you godly advice. She should pray with you and hold you accountable as a wife and in your areas of personal weakness.

This woman must be a committed, growing Christian, a woman who will always support your marriage, who can take whatever you say, no matter how intense, angry, or personal, and not freak out and think less of you. She can hear you "dump" your frustrations about your IA and not think less of him. She can keep all your secrets and not tell another living soul (including her husband) what you share with her. She will love you and be there for you. She will also see you as her best friend and use you as her confidante and supporter.

It is ideal to have a best friend who lives close to you. That way she is available and your connection to her can grow stronger. She cannot be a family member. A relative usually takes your side and cannot be objective. Plus, telling a relative everything about your husband will likely damage his ongoing relationship with your family.

If you don't have such a friend, start praying and looking. Until you find her, use a long-distance friend or a wise, caring woman at your church. Perhaps one of the pastors' or leaders' wives can temporarily come alongside you. Your kindred spirit is out there, in your church, Bible study, or neighborhood. In His time God will lead the two of you together.

A Small Group of Friends and Family

Along with God and a best friend, it is a good idea to develop a small support group of good friends and family members. Try to get at least two or three. Don't express all your emotions and tell them everything, as you would with your one bosom friend. But you can share quite a bit about your marital struggles. Let them know you are married to an intimacy avoider. This information won't shock them; they will probably say, "Join the club." Let them know about the Husband Transformation Strategy you are following, and give them regular updates on your progress.

I hate to state the obvious, but this group should be all female. Whether relatives, friends, or coworkers, the men in your life are almost certainly IAs, so they won't get it.

This small group of supporters will serve you in two ways:

1. They will handle the overflow emotional needs that your best friend won't be able to meet on her own. If you don't have a best friend yet or your best friend isn't available, you can call your small group members. After you have talked to God and your best

friend, and still need to vent and receive encouragement, call these supporters.

2. Each member of your small group should regularly pray for you and your husband. Give these prayer warriors regular, specific updates and requests so they know exactly how to pray. Most of the time these friends and relatives will pray on their own for you. At other times pray with individual supporters in person or by phone.

If possible, meet with your small group once every two weeks or once a month to pray. Of course you'll be praying for each of them and their needs as well.

Your Church Family

You need a local church that will support you emotionally and spiritually as you work to change your husband. You will need a church where you have two or three close female friends who will be part of your husband-changing support team. You need a church that teaches the Bible from the pulpit, offers Sunday school or women's Bible study, and some kind of small group where you can receive encouragement and emotional connections. You also need a church where you can worship God and serve Him with your gifts. While not essential, it is preferable that it have strong women's, men's, and marriage ministries. A church with these programs can meet your relational needs, expose your husband to good Christian male models, and provide biblical teaching on how to build a great marriage. The foundation is set. Now, on to step two!

STEP TWO

THIS IS EXACTLY THE KIND OF HUSBAND I NEED YOU TO BE

Chapter 4

The Man Who
Knew Too Little

I SN'T IT INCREDIBLE how often your husband just doesn't get it? He walks around in his own little world, blissfully unaware of you and your needs. It's a real puzzle. He appears to have an IQ in the normal range. He can groom and dress himself without assistance, is competent at his job, and speaks the same language as you. Yet despite these abilities, in many of your daily interactions he completely misses what is so painfully obvious to you. He just doesn't get it.

Read these scenarios. I'll bet you'll recognize them.

Sex is always the answer

You and your husband had an argument twenty minutes ago. It did not end well. You're angry, hurt, and feel totally misunderstood. You've gone to bed early. The bedroom is dark and you're curled up on your side of the bed, nursing your wounds. He comes into the room, crawls into bed, and snuggles softly against you. You turn to him, expecting an apology and an attempt to talk through the conflict. Instead he wants sex! The only sounds he makes are grunts. Is he some kind of an animal? Yes. Does he really think that sex will solve this problem and make everything better? Yes, he does.

Mr. Romance

Several days ago you and your husband were talking about your upcoming anniversary. You sensed that he didn't seem too excited. He couldn't come up with any ideas for what to do. So you said, "Well, honey, it isn't really necessary to do anything special." Yet today is the day and, sure enough, *he didn't do anything special*. No card. No roses. No gift. No dinner out, although he did bring home a pizza. What kind of a clueless wonder would imagine that you would be satisfied with takeout on your anniversary? Your husband, that's who.

The sensitive male

You're telling your husband about your rotten day at the office, highlighted by your male boss treating you badly in front of several coworkers. You go into detail, paying particular attention to your feelings of anger, hurt, and humiliation. Instead of helping you feel understood and offering comfort, your husband responds by saying he can see your boss's point of view. He informs you these things happen in offices everywhere, that it's no big deal, and your boss was probably just stressed out. He looks thoughtful for a moment. You think maybe he has realized his mistake. You ask if he has anything else to say and he responds, "Yeah. What's for dinner?" Your moan of anguish and frustration can be heard four houses away.

It's PMS, isn't it?

It's been a long day. Your considerate husband forgot to call the mechanic about your car. Plus he forgot the two items you wanted from the grocery store, but he did manage to come home with his favorite ice cream and a package of beef jerky. Later he commented that your chicken was a tad overdone, he (not the chicken) didn't help with the dishes, and he spent an hour in front of his computer. You've just tried to start a conversation with him, but he's focused on the TV and didn't hear a word you said. You go into the kitchen, slam a few cupboards, and begin to cry. He comes in looking for a snack, notices you, and says, "What's wrong? Is it PMS, honey?" You want to scream, "No, it's not PMS! It's NBS, honey! No Brain Syndrome!"

It's a Man Thing

Situations such as these when your man doesn't get it are not isolated occurrences. They happen all the time. He doesn't see what's really going on and what you need from him. As my good friend John Louer likes to say, "I'm working with very small tools." Your husband has very small tools. He doesn't know much about relationships. He doesn't grasp your basic needs, why you get upset, or what he can do to make you feel secure and loved.

The trouble is he is sure he knows what your needs are and that he is doing a great job meeting them. When he fails to meet your needs and you get frustrated and angry, he doesn't blame himself. He blames you. Thousands of my male IA clients have given me the same message: "Doc, I love her. I'm doing my best. I'm doing everything I can to make her happy. I don't know why she gets all hurt and angry. It must be a woman thing: hormones, being oversensitive, or just expecting too much. She's awfully tough to please."

With their wives sitting right there in my therapy office, I have asked these same husbands to tell me about their wives' needs. Without fail they launch confidently into their recitation of what they think their wife needs. And every husband (the whole bunch), much to their shock and dismay, have been wrong. I mean, dead wrong. Not-even-close wrong. When she responds with what she really needs, the reaction is typically the husband's mouth hanging open in surprise.

It's a Woman Thing

It isn't just the husband who exhibits surprise during these sessions, though. As she tells him her needs, the wife is genuinely surprised that he doesn't know. Almost every wife of an IA I have counseled in therapy has told me that she firmly believes her husband knows her needs. So when he doesn't meet them, it creates a double whammy to her solar plexus. Not only is she hurt because of unmet needs, but also she feels angry and insulted because she thought he *knew* her needs and deliberately chose to ignore them.

When I ask these wives why they are so sure their husbands know their needs, they all say basically the same thing: "How could he *not* know? It's obvious what my needs are every day. He can tell by just watching me. Doesn't he have eyes, ears, and a brain? There is no way he could miss my needs that much. No, he knows what I need, and he just refuses to come through."

When I ask the man to identify his spouse's needs and he can't, it dawns on the wife that he really doesn't know. Just as I illustrated in the four vignettes at the beginning of this chapter, he doesn't get it. I explain to the wife that men are almost universally oblivious to social cues that wives find obvious. While she thinks she is sending clear signals about what she would like him to do in a situation, she isn't. She is sending subtle, coded signals that only other women understand. But she is not dealing with a woman; she is dealing with an IA of the opposite sex. That means there is zero chance he will get the message.

Not only does your man miss what you need in specific situations when you think words aren't necessary, he also doesn't even get it when you tell him your needs right to his face. The following list gives some insight into how this all goes wrong:

- Maybe you weren't as clear as you thought you were. Women tend to be too subtle. They like men to connect the dots and figure it out without too much help. Men can't connect the dots. Men don't even know there are dots to connect.

- Maybe he wasn't listening. Men are notoriously poor listeners. They tune out, listen selectively, get distracted, or get lost in your words and don't want to admit it.

- Maybe he forgot what you said about your needs. Men have terrible memories, especially with personal items. They can remember financial reports, sports trivia, and other facts that do not improve the quality of their marriages.

- Maybe you spoke to him with too much emotion. When a woman gets too emotionally intense, a man's brain short-circuits and her message gets garbled. He screens it out, because he can only focus on *how* she is saying it. All he thinks is, "Man, she's way too intense. She's lost it."

- Maybe you pushed him too hard and he feels backed into a corner. When a man feels controlled by his woman, he clams up and gets very defensive. He digs in his heels and won't give her what she wants, no matter how reasonable her request.

- Maybe he didn't believe you. As crazy as it sounds, men have a bad habit of thinking *they* know what is best for their wives. It's possible he thinks his wife doesn't know what she really needs, but that *he* knows. Dumb? Sure. Does it happen? All the time.

As you can see, there are a lot of things that can and do go wrong when you attempt to communicate your needs to your husband. Some of it is your fault and some of it is his. Some of it is just because wires get crossed in the inherent gender differences that are part of male-female conversations. Whatever the reasons, your message doesn't get across, and he has no idea what your needs are.

If You Want Him to Get It, Give It to Him

A foundational step in my Husband Transformation Strategy is the crystal clear communication of your needs as a wife to your husband. You do it because he doesn't know your needs. This step is a springboard for the remaining five steps. The Bible teaches this: when there is a stumbling block between you and a brother, your Christian duty is to go to that person and seek to resolve the problem (Matt. 5:23–24; 18:15–17).

When you're in this one-on-one meeting with your husband, you will be "speaking the truth in love" (Eph. 4:15). Forget subtlety. Check your emotional intensity at the door. Make no effort to push him for a response. You must deliver the message of your needs in a way your husband can receive and understand it. You must be blunt. Direct. Specific. Rational. You must spell it out for him in black-and-white detail.

The real beauty—and power—of my approach is that you're not only going to be communicating what *you* need. You're going to be communicating what *God* says you need. There is a world of a difference. Husbands—even Christian husbands—resist when their wives ask them to meet needs. Husbands have a much harder time resisting when their wives point to what God commands them to do as husbands.

You'll lay before your man God's biblical instructions for husbands. You'll take him through a mini-seminar on his biblical job description. Remember, this isn't primarily about you and him. First and foremost it is about God and him. If he obeys

God's guidelines on his role as a husband, he benefits. God will be pleased and bless him. You will benefit because, for the first time, he will meet the deepest needs of your heart. Your children will benefit because they will feel secure and learn how to build a great marriage. Those around you will benefit because they will see what a Christ-centered marriage looks like. Here is exactly what I want you to do:

Set up the first meeting

Go to your husband, sit him down, take his hands in yours, look into his eyes, and in the most serious tone you can muster, say these words:

> _____ (his name),
>
> There is something very important I want to talk to you about. I'm not ready to do it now, because I'm still sorting through some things. I want the kids to be out of the house when we talk. It needs to be just the two of us. Let's meet in three days.

After scheduling this meeting, go on about your business. He may ask, "What is this is all about?" Don't tell him anything. He has to wait until the meeting. Spend the next three days acting cool, reserved, and a little pulled back. Nothing dramatic. Just remain in a quiet, contemplative mood. You want him to wonder, even worry, about what you are going to say. You want this meeting to make a demonstrable impact on his life.

The first meeting

At the first meeting say these words to your husband:

> _____ (his name),
>
> I have been thinking and praying a lot about our marriage these past few weeks. The truth is, I'm not happy. I have really important, deep needs that only you can meet

as my husband, and you're not meeting them. That's partly your fault. It's also partly my fault.

I realize that I haven't made my needs clear to you. You can't meet them if you don't know exactly what they are. I have read this book (show him my book), and I think it can help us build a terrific marriage. I have decided to follow all the steps described by Dr. Clarke and would love for you to join me so we can work on our marriage together.

The first step is for me to clearly communicate to you the needs I have as your wife. Please read chapters 5, 6, and 7 in the coming week. In these chapters Dr. Clarke explains what the Bible says about the husband's role in marriage. Honey, I have read these chapters, and, believe me, they paint the picture of the husband I need you to be. Please understand that it's not just *me* saying that I have these needs. It's *God* saying that I have these needs.

I want to meet in a week to discuss these chapters. Feel free to write your thoughts and reactions in the book or on a piece of paper. I particularly want you to tell me how you think you're doing in the role of a biblical husband (as stated in the book). What time next week will work for you?

Don't show much emotion as you deliver this message. The more cool, calm, and collected you can be, the better the chance that he will focus on what you're saying and act on it. It is a good idea to put the message in your own words so they sound more personal. You might want to write down what you say to him or refer to notes. It can be easy to forget what you intend to say in the intensity and awkwardness of the situation.

Of course you will have already read chapters 5, 6, and 7 before this meeting. In fact, you should have read the entire book. If he chooses to read more during the week, fine. The more he reads, the better. Men don't like to read, though, so don't get your hopes up. You will be lucky if he reads these three chapters.

It is very possible your husband will be blown away by what you say at this first meeting. He may be shocked or confused—maybe a little angry. If he is a typical man, he thinks your marriage is great. Now you are saying it is not. He may have considerable trouble adjusting to this reality. If he wants to, let him discuss his feelings with you. Whenever a man wants to talk, that is a good thing. He may want to ask questions, find out what is going on, and get some reassurance that everything will be OK. Let him talk, but don't give out too much information. *Do not* reassure him, because that will stop any momentum or motivation. If you say things are "OK" or "will be OK," that signals him that he doesn't have to change. So he won't. You will kill any chance of success before you can start.

Simply direct him to chapters 5, 6, and 7. Tell him he will find the answers to his questions in those chapters. This will make it more likely that he will read them—carefully. What you want him to recognize at this point in the process is that he is not meeting your needs.

The second meeting

If he chooses not to read those three chapters, the second meeting will be short. Express your anger and disappointment that he didn't care enough about you to read them. Do not lose your temper. Do not raise your voice. Just move on to the next step. Tell him you have something you want to read to him and schedule a meeting to be held in three or four days.

If he has read the chapters, thank him and ask him to share his reactions. Based on the three biblical roles, ask him how he thinks he is doing as your husband. What he says will reveal where his heart is and his willingness to change. Hopefully he will be willing to admit that he is falling short of God's standards for husbands and that he wants to do better.

Repeat that these chapters describe the kind of husband you need him to be. Tell him you know he can become such a husband, and you don't expect him to do it alone. You want to work with him every step of the way. Share with him that the next step will be you reading something to him in a few days. Schedule that meeting.

Your letter of needs

In your third meeting you will read him an intensely personal and brutally honest letter containing the most accurate, vivid description possible of your needs. It will be a tough, no-frills letter. There will be no sunshiny positives. No "I hope I don't offend him," or "I'd hate to hurt his feelings." Don't use "dear," "honey," or "I love you" expressions. You want him to know this is serious business.

You will be painstakingly specific in presenting your needs—leave no room for doubt. You will lead him to water and you will make him drink. What you are giving him is a detailed map to your heart. After you have read this letter and handed it to him, he will never again have an excuse for not knowing your needs. To remind him that he answers ultimately to God for his role as husband, weave into your letter the main points from chapters 5, 6, and 7. Within this biblical framework you will reveal what you, as a unique woman and *his wife*, need from him.

Below is a sample letter containing the points I recommend including. In composing yours, use your own words and distinctive style of communication. Tell him right up front that you do not want him to interrupt as you read your letter. If he wants to ask questions or make comments, he can do so after you have finished reading.

_____ (his name,)

I don't want you to have any doubt about what I need from you. So I have written this letter spelling out exactly what my needs are as your wife. After I read it, I will hand it to you. I want you to keep it in a safe place—permanently. If you ever forget my needs, just pull out the letter and read it again.

First, and most important, God says you are to be *a godly man*. My deepest need as your wife is to see you in a growing, vital relationship with Jesus Christ. If you're not walking closely with Jesus, you won't have the power to meet any of my needs. Please do these things to keep your spiritual life on track:

- Have a daily quiet time with the Lord in which you pray and read your Bible.

- Be accountable in a meeting at least once a week to a godly man for your spiritual growth and role as my husband.

- Attend a men's conference once a year.

- Attend church with the kids and me every week. I also need you to be my spiritual leader. Please make sure we pray together for at least five minutes, three times a week. Please meet with me once a week, for fifteen or twenty minutes, so each of us can share what's going on in our spiritual lives. We can help each other grow spiritually. Dr. Clarke has another book, *A Marriage After God's Own Heart*, that teaches couples how to spiritually bond. I want us to read it together and apply the principles of bonding in Christ as a couple.

- I need you to lead once-a-week family devotions. I would be happy to work with you in preparing for these meetings. I want a Bible passage read and discussed, an opportunity for family concerns to be raised, and time at the end for prayer.

Second, God says you are to be *my lover*. I know you love me, but it's essential you love me in the specific ways *I* need to be loved. Only I can define how I feel loved. Communication is very important to me. I need you to set aside thirty minutes on four days of each week, as early in the evening as possible, for the two of us to talk. I want to talk in the den without any distractions: no kids, no television, no computer, no newspaper, and no answering the door or the telephone. I need you to come to me every evening we've scheduled to talk, and say, "It's time for our talk."

When we talk, I need you to listen to me in the active way Dr. Clarke explains: eye contact, body language, feeding back key words and phrases, identifying my emotions, and reacting to what I say. Show interest in my life and the people and events in it. Ask me questions about what I do and how I feel.

I also need you to talk to me. I can't tell you how much I long to hear what's going on inside of you: your feelings, your stresses, what God is teaching you every day, and your hopes and dreams. Please take a small pad with you wherever you go each day, and jot down things you would like to share during our talks. When we have a conflict, I need you (and me too) to follow Dr. Clarke's rules for a fair fight: one of us at a time, listen and reflect, build understanding first, see it as a process that happens in stages, and come to a decision. Let's practice these rules together. I don't mind you walking away from a conflict if you're too angry to continue, but I need you to *come back* so we can keep talking until we've resolved it.

When I'm upset, just let me vent and help me feel understood. It's when I'm hurt and angry that I really need you to listen and reflect. Just feed back to me what *I'm* saying and feeling. Please, no male logic. That just makes me angrier. Even though I know it's difficult for you, I need you to apologize and keep letting me talk when you've hurt my feelings. Don't walk away permanently. I want you to come back and comfort me and reassure me of your love. Let me talk it all out.

I'm writing my basic, fundamental needs in this letter. These are my "core" needs that are an integral part of who I am. These needs don't change. But I have other needs that change from day to day. I want you to do your best to meet these needs as well. Part of *understanding* and *respecting* me is to ask me every day what I need from you. This is how you can meet these fluctuating needs. Please ask me twice a day what my needs are—in the morning and after work as our evening begins. The mere action of asking me what I need will make me feel very loved. Plus I'll tell you specifically what you can do for me, so you'll be able to target and meet these daily needs.

I need you to *romance* me. Ask me out on a date once a week. Half the time please get the babysitter and plan the date. At least once a month do something with me on the date that I would like to do: walk on the beach, see a chick flick, go to a craft fair, or walk through the mall. I also need daily physical affection from you. Not sexually intimate touching like we do in foreplay, but nonsexual touching: kissing, hugging, holding my hand, or giving me a neck massage.

I need to hear "I love you" at least once a day. Praise me for who I am—my character traits or what I do for you and the kids. About once every two or three weeks get me a card and write a special note in it.

Third, God says you are to be a *servant leader* like Jesus. Please do your share of the household chores. I will feel loved and have more energy when you do your chores. Ask me every day what needs to be done around the house.

Let's make decisions together in all major areas: parenting, finances, major purchases, home repairs, our spiritual lives, time spent with our respective in-laws, and so on. Please discuss significant decisions with me thoroughly, pray with me about them, and then we'll settle on a course of action.

Well, that's about it. I know this is a lot to take in and digest. But this is what God wants you to do and what I need you to do. I'm sorry for not being clear on what my needs are until now.

I have to admit that I've been unhappy because you haven't been meeting enough of my needs. I have felt unloved, and I have lost respect for you. I have not felt close to you emotionally, so I haven't been too interested in our physical relationship. Sex is more of a chore for me than the joyful, passionate experience God intends it to be. If you don't meet my needs, I cannot be a good wife to you in any area.

I hope and pray that this letter begins a process that will change our marriage and bring us much closer. I don't expect you to be perfect, just committed to working hard to meet my needs and become the husband I know you can be. I will be following Dr. Clarke's strategy. If you want to know his entire strategy, that would be great. Read the book, and we'll discuss each step as we implement it. If you don't want to read any more than chapters 5, 6, and 7, that is fine. I will do the steps and let you know what I'm doing and why as we go along.

Thank you for listening. I don't expect you to give me your reaction now. You'll need time to process all this. Let me know when you're ready to talk about it.

_____ (your name)

When you finish reading, hand him the letter. If he has no immediate response—and he probably won't—get up and walk away. If he wants to talk about it, he will find you. Now what follows are the chapters that present the Bible's teaching about the three roles of a husband. Though they are written primarily for your husband, I want you to read them. After that we will continue reviewing the rest of my strategy.

Chapter 5

God Says:
Be a Godly Man

O K, ALL YOU husbands who are reading this (most at your wife's direction), I have a pretty good idea of what you are thinking: "This Clarke guy has some nerve calling me an intimacy avoider. Who does he think he is?" Let me explain who I am and my goals for this book. Remember, I am a man, so I understand the male makeup.

Most men are intimacy avoiders. I am an intimacy avoider; or at least, I used to be. As men we hold our thoughts and feelings inside and don't discuss personal feelings—with our wives or anyone else. Ring any bells? This ingrained style of not letting anyone, especially our wives, see who we are inside makes us IAs.

I know you love your wife, more than anyone else on this earth. But if you are not talking with her regularly on a personal level, I have some bad news: *she doesn't feel loved by you*. This is tragic, because the number-one desire of her heart is to be close to you and to know you as no one else does. She wants to hear you talk honestly and openly about your life, work, relationship with her, walk with God, children, hopes and dreams, and the things that are important to her—this is what she has always dreamed about. To be denied such fulfillment devastates her.

That is why she bought this book. That's why she asked you to read this chapter and the two following it. She wants you to join her in building a better, closer, deeper relationship. She understands that what she is asking won't come easy. In fact, it will be quite difficult—one of the most difficult things you have ever done. But she is hoping and praying that you will love her enough to do it.

For years I held back with my wife, Sandy. I talked with her about only safe, superficial topics. Again and again she tried to get me to lower my wall and let her see inside to what I really thought and felt, but I wouldn't do it. I didn't think she needed to know the personal things about me. Man, was I wrong. I was hurting her and making my precious wife feel unhappy and unfulfilled in our marriage. Hiding behind my walls and holding her at arm's length was squeezing the life out of Sandy and our marriage. And it was my fault! We still *loved* each other; we just weren't *in love*. The fun, romance, exciting sex, and passion had disappeared from our marriage. Maybe that is where you are today.

I finally figured out how to open up and let Sandy see inside so she could know the real me. I won't lie to you. It wasn't easy, but it has been worth the effort. Sandy and I are closer and hap- pier now than we've ever been. Our marriage has taken off. It all started with me understanding her needs. Although I thought I knew, I didn't have a clue. I did three things to figure them out: 1) I talked to Sandy many times, 2) I listened to thousands of wives in therapy telling me what they needed, and 3) I studied the Bible.

Do you know what I discovered? The needs Sandy and all these wives mentioned were the same ones God describes in the Bible. God knows your woman intimately. He knows what she needs. If you follow His instructions about how to be a husband, you will meet your wife's most important needs. In chapters 5, 6, and 7 I will show you the kind of husband God wants you to be and your wife needs you to be.

Being a Husband Ain't Easy

What is the greatest challenge in life for a man? Climbing Mount Everest? Winning a triathlon? Building a successful business? Becoming president of the United States? No. No. No. And no. These challenges are a piece of cake compared to life's ultimate man test: *living with a woman*. Women are wonderful, fascinating, and exciting. They are also difficult to please, confusing, and unpredictable. At least they are to men.

Picture this scene. It is a weekday morning, and a man and his wife are preparing to go their separate ways. He says, "Good-bye, honey." She says, "When will you be home tonight?" She's asked a dangerous question. It's deep water, but the man doesn't realize it. So he replies, "Oh, I don't know, around six thirty."

In his mind *around* six thirty means *around* six thirty—a ballpark estimate, a range. That could mean six forty, six forty-five, or seven. He is giving her his best guess. The woman, being a woman, zeroes in on six thirty. For her that is neither an estimate nor a range but a fixed point in time. He said six thirty, and six thirty is carved in stone. It is a guarantee, a promise, a deal! She doesn't say any of this to her husband, of course. That would be too easy. But she is thinking it.

So off to work the poor man goes, with no idea that he has made a deal. If he comes home at six forty, he is late, and she will be cold and irritated. There will be no kiss at the front door. If he comes home at six forty-five, he is *really* late. She will be angry. His dinner will be...put away. If he wanders in at seven or later, look out. He is a liar and has broken a promise! She will be outraged and hurt. It's going to be a long, frosty night, Bubba.

Sound familiar, men?

Husbands, this is just one example of why we need help in dealing with a woman. We are out of our league! We need some kind of a plan or strategy for living with a woman in an understanding and intimate way. I have good news. God, the Creator of man and woman, has provided that strategy. The principles He sets forth in the Bible on how to be a husband have not changed in thousands of years. They still apply and still work. In fact, they are the only principles that work.

God requires that a husband carry out four critical roles:

1. Be a godly man.

2. Be a lover.

3. Be a romancer.

4. Be a leader.

In the remainder of this chapter I will cover the essentials of the first point. Don't bail out on me too quickly though. The other three points that follow in the next two chapters are equally important. I know; you don't like to read. But you better if you want your marriage to improve. So stick with me.

Be a Godly Man

Don't look to society for guidance on how to be a man. Look to Scripture. Society says be good-looking, be financially successful, and be a sexual superstar. The basic message is: "Think of yourself, because, after all, you're really something special." In the world's eyes the way to happiness is making a ton of money, buying all the male toys, and having sex with as many women as possible.

Is there pleasure in following society's blueprint for male achievement and success? Sure. Does it provide lasting joy, peace, and fulfillment? Hardly. Take a close look at the icons of male success in business, entertainment, or sports. You will see men destroying themselves with addictions to alcohol, drugs, and sex. You will see men whose lives are littered with failed marriages, destroyed relationships, and deeply scarred children.

This is success? I'll tell you what it is; it's stupid. Actually it is worse than that. It is a lie straight from Satan himself, the great deceiver. Go ahead and chase society's goals for manhood if you want, but they won't work. Never have; never will. All they are good for is breaking your wife's heart, damaging your children, and leaving you miserable.

Follow Scripture

Scripture says love God and be like Christ. These two verses say it all:

> "Teacher, which is the great commandment in the Law?" And He said to him, 'You shall love the Lord your God with all your heart, and with all your soul, and with all your mind.'"
> —MATTHEW 22:36–37

> Therefore be imitators of God, as beloved children; and walk in love, just as Christ also loved you, and gave Himself up for us.
> —EPHESIANS 5:1–2

We are to love God with everything we have and live as Jesus Christ lived. This is the definition of a godly man. Men, how does your life match this definition? There have been times in my life when I wasn't even close. Oh, I was a Christian and went to church, but I wasn't in love with God. I wasn't living like Jesus. I still hung on to certain areas of sin and lived the way I wanted to live. Maybe that is how you are living now. If you can honestly admit that you are not the man God wants you to be, then you have some work to do.

You Won't Believe the Benefits

When you love God and walk in a close relationship with Jesus, you will find the power to live life in the successful way God has planned. It will make all the difference in your personal life and career and especially in your relationship with your wife. Since this is a marriage book, I will zero in on the last part of that sentence. The Bible says that God will richly bless the marriage and family of a godly man:

> Your wife shall be like a fruitful vine, within your house, your children like olive plants around your table. Behold, for thus shall the man be blessed who fears the LORD.
> —PSALM 128:3–4

Your wife will be thrilled with your spiritual growth. I guarantee it. It is one of the deepest desires—and needs—of every Christian wife. It is tied for first place (or even slightly ahead) with her need to emotionally connect with you. In my therapy practice and at marriage seminars, wife after wife after wife has said, "Oh, I wish my husband was a godly man!"

When you are a godly man, your wife will love and respect you in ways you didn't believe possible. You have heard the old saying, "When Momma ain't happy, ain't nobody happy." You know that is true. When your wife isn't happy, it makes you miserable, doesn't it? When you are spiritually healthy, she will be happy, fulfilled, and at peace. Feeling great about you, she will return the favor. So you will be happy too.

On a practical level being a godly man will give you the power to be a good husband. Humanly speaking, you can't do it. Not just because women are so hard to live with (even though that is true), but because what God requires of us as husbands is so difficult. Have you read Ephesians lately? Take a look:

> Husbands, love your wives, just as Christ also loved the church and gave Himself up for her.
> —EPHESIANS 5:25

Whoa! I mean, whoa! How can you love your wife like this under your own strength? You can't! No way.

For years I tried to love Sandy in an Ephesians 5:25 way on my own, and it didn't work. I finally got past my ignorance and pride and realized that being a good husband is a supernatural job. Once I had God's help, I did a much better job.

God knows your woman better than you ever will. He knows what she needs. As you get closer and closer to Him, He will work through you to love her.

Come to Christ

To be a godly man, you need to know God. And the only way to know God is to know Jesus Christ. Let me give you the straight facts on how to begin a relationship with God through His Son, Jesus.

You are a sinner. So am I. So is everyone. You have made plenty of mistakes in your life, haven't you? Well, even one little mistake, one sin, separates you from God. On your own there is no way to reach a holy and perfect God. Romans 3:23 drives this point home: "For all have sinned and fall short of the glory of God."

God could have left you in your sin, condemned to never know Him, die, and go to hell. But He didn't do that. God loves you so much that He sent His only Son, Jesus, to Earth to die for your sins. Jesus paid your price, the price of your sins: death, eternal separation from God and heaven.

> For the wages of sin is death, but the free gift of God is eternal life in Christ Jesus our Lord.
>
> —ROMANS 6:23

Here is the truth you must believe to know God and become a Christian:

> ...that Christ died for our sins according to the Scriptures, and that He was buried, and that He was raised on the third day according to the Scriptures.
>
> —1 CORINTHIANS 15:3–4

Do you want all your sins, the ones you have already done and the ones you will do the rest of your life—the sins of your whole life—wiped away? Do you want to know God personally? Do you want God's power to live your life here on the earth? Do you want to go to heaven when you die? If you answered yes to these questions, then you're ready to come to Christ.

Repeat the following prayer to begin a relationship with God:

God, I'm a sinner. I've made many mistakes and sinned in my life. I know that my sin separates me from You. I can't reach You on my own. Thank You for sending Jesus as the only way for me to get to know You. I believe Jesus died on the cross for my sins. I believe Jesus rose from the dead, proving He is God and has the power to forgive my sins. I'm tired of living my life my way. I now give my life to You, God. Amen.

Grow in Christ

I see too many husbands who have come to Christ and know Christ, yet they aren't growing in Christ. I have been there too, so I am not throwing any stones. Real men are men who aren't perfect, but who are maturing spiritually and growing in their walk with Jesus: "Be on the alert, stand firm in the faith, act like men, be strong" (1 Cor. 16:13).

If you want to be a real man, be a man who is growing in Christ. Attend church regularly. Go to Sunday school and build relationships with other Christians. Find a place in your church to serve others. Go to a men's conference at least once a year.

Spend time each day alone with God. It can be ten minutes or thirty. It can be early in the morning, at lunch, or in the evening. Talk to God in prayer. Adore Him and worship Him for who He is. Thank and praise Him for what He has done for you and your family. Talk to Him about your life, feelings, concerns, and stress.

Ask Him to guide you. End with requests, but be sure never to make all your prayer a list of requests.

Listen to God too. Through the Holy Spirit He will find ways to communicate with you. Just be quiet in God's presence and see what happens. The main way God will speak to you is through the Bible. Read a verse or two during your quiet time with God. Meditate on what you read. Every time you read the Bible, God is speaking to you.

Be Accountable to One Man

Once every week or two, in a face-to-face meeting, find a man who will hold you accountable in all the important areas of your life: husband, father, career, areas of temptation, and your relationship with Jesus. Few men have a relationship like this. Be the exception. It will change your life. I guarantee it. Moses had Aaron and Joshua. David had Jonathan. Paul had Barnabas. Whom do you have?

Over the past twelve years I have had Rocky Glisson. Rocky is my best friend. Every Saturday morning at a local diner, unless one of us is sick or I am out of town speaking, we sit down for an accountability meeting. We go over the preceding week and ask each other the tough questions. I know Rocky's weaknesses—the areas where he tends to sin. And Rocky knows mine.

Rocky is my supporter, encourager, confronter. He is the guy I go to war with against Satan and his schemes to ruin my life. Rocky keeps me away from sins that can destroy my marriage, my family, and me. One of those areas is work. ("Hello, my name is Dave, and I'm a workaholic.") When Rocky sees me getting carried away, he will bark, "David, you're in the workaholic zone again. Stop it! Cut back, or I'll have to hurt you." Most importantly Rocky keeps me on track spiritually. He asks me how I'm doing in my walk with Jesus. Am I having my daily quiet time? Am I reading my Bible? What did God teach me this past week?

In every meeting we share our triumphs, joys, worries, and failures. We end every session by praying for the specific requests we have brought to the table.

Look for a man your age or older who loves the Lord and is an excellent husband, a man who has figured out how to love his wife and meet her needs, and a man who has learned how to communicate openly and honestly with his spouse. Ask him to teach you how to be a great husband.

Rocky has made a huge difference in my life. Because of our accountability relationship, I am a better husband, father, and psychologist. Best of all I am closer to Jesus. Find a Rocky. Start praying and looking. God will lead you to him.

Lead Your Wife Spiritually

Part of being a godly man is leading your wife spiritually. Scripture teaches that the husband is the leader in the marriage relationship:

> For the husband is the head of the wife, as Christ also is the head of the church, He Himself being the Savior of the body. But as the church is subject to Christ, so also the wives ought to be to their husbands in everything.
> —EPHESIANS 5:23–24

The husband is to lead in *everything*. (Of course, I'm not referring to the myriad special talents, abilities, skills of wives, which are too numerous to list, as with the "excellent wife" described in Proverbs 31.) Everything means everything, including the spiritual area. Ephesians 5:25–31 describes a husband who leads by caring for his wife in a compassionate, tender, and attentive way. Your job as a loving leader is to make sure every facet of your precious wife's life is healthy. Her spiritual life is, in fact, the most important part of who she is. From a biblical perspective her deepest individual need is for you to help her maintain a close, growing relationship with Jesus Christ.

How can you do this? By scheduling regular times of prayer and spiritual sharing with your wife. Is this tough? Is it ever! As a husband this is one of the hardest things I do. I often feel uncomfortable, threatened, awkward, and incompetent. Even after ten years of working on a spiritual bond with Sandy, Satan tries to block us every step of the way. He knows that these spiritual bonding behaviors are essential to a healthy marriage. He knows that he can't destroy our marriage if we regularly discuss our spiritual lives and pray together.

Is it worth it? It sure is. Sandy and I are stronger and closer than ever. Joining together spiritually for just a few minutes a week has revived our passion and intimacy. It is still hard to lead Sandy spiritually, but I am going to keep on keeping on. It is what God wants me to do and what Sandy needs me to do. It is keeping our marriage alive and well.

I want you to do two things. First, sit down with your wife every Saturday or Sunday evening and schedule three five-minute prayer sessions for the coming week. If you don't schedule them, you won't do them. When the appointed time comes, go to your wife and ask her to pray with you. Sit down in a quiet, private place in your home, just the two of you, and list prayer requests. Then hold hands and pray one at a time.

At first, you will likely pray for safe topics: your children, family, health concerns, church, and people you know. As you go along, you will start sharing and praying for more personal, intimate issues: your worries, fears, dreams, spiritual weaknesses, God's guidance, and protection against Satan's attacks.

The second thing, which you should schedule the same way you do prayer, is to meet with your wife at the end of every week for a spiritual evaluation. Because life is so busy, this is a great way to stay connected spiritually. For a total of fifteen or twenty minutes each of you should share what happened in your spiritual lives in the past week, what you learned in daily quiet times, how you applied the Bible, and what God taught you. Share your spiritual victories and defeats.

If you want to learn more about how to spiritually bond as a husband and wife, read my book *A Marriage After God's Own Heart*. However, these two spiritual activities will get you headed in the right direction. Don't think you have to be a spiritual giant to do this or that you really need to know what you're doing. Just do it. You won't be alone. God will help you. When she can see you are making an honest effort, your wife is much more likely to be patient, kind, and to work with you as you bond spiritually.

Again, men, don't be a godly man just for your wife. True, this will be very good for her, but that isn't the real point. Do it for God. *He* wants you to grow spiritually and to lead your wife in developing closer spiritual bonds.

Chapter 6

God Says:
Be a Lover

BEING A GOOD lover is all about listening to, talking with, understanding, and respecting your wife. It is *not* about sex, which is quite likely the first thought that popped into your head when you read the word *lover*. Hey, don't get me wrong. Sex with your wife is important, very important. I want you to enjoy a regular, passionate sex life with your dear wife.

However, being a great sexual partner doesn't make you a great lover. In fact, it is just the opposite. Being a great, biblical lover will make you a great sex partner. It will make your wife a great sex partner as well.

Now that I have your attention, here is the big idea of this chapter: *A great lover is a husband who meets his wife's emotional needs.* That is the Bible's bottom line regarding marriage. That is what God wants you to do. Believe me, it is what your wife is hoping, praying for, and dreaming about. When you learn how, the blessings of God will shower you and your wife. You will become best friends and as close and intimate as two people can be. As a result, your sex life will be nothing short of terrific.

I know you don't know how to be a great lover. Yet. That is nothing to be embarrassed about. For the first fifteen years of my marriage I didn't know how either. I am going to teach you what I learned, so let's get to it.

Ephesians 5 and the One-Two Punch

Remember the marital passage from Ephesians 5:25? Paul winds up and hits every husband right in the stomach with a dramatic command: "Husbands, love your wives, just as Christ also loved the church and gave Himself up for her."

This is the highest possible standard of love! Christ gave everything, including His life, for the church. You must do the same by loving your wife in a sacrificial, unconditional way. That means totally focusing on meeting her needs. Did you get that? In case you didn't, Paul repeats and amplifies the message with a brutal punch right to the jaw three verses later:

> So husbands ought also to love their own wives as their own bodies. He who loves his own wife loves himself; for no one ever hated his own flesh, but nourishes and cherishes it, just as Christ also does the church.
> —Ephesians 5:28–29

Your job is to love your wife by *nourishing* and *cherishing* her. Show her the most tender care and concern, just as you do for your own body. The same way Jesus does for His church. Your role in marriage is not about meeting your needs. It boils down to meeting your wife's needs. Through His servant Paul, in Ephesians 5, God commands you to meet your wife's needs. In the way only a husband can. Not to try. To do it. And some of her most important needs are in the emotional arena.

Listen to Your Wife

The first step in being a real lover is to learn to listen to your wife. Answer this true-false statement: Men, by nature, are exceptional, excellent listeners. You know the answer, don't you? *False!* Only one man was born an excellent listener: Jesus Christ. The rest of us have to learn. And we must learn, because there isn't a wife in the world who can feel genuinely loved and cherished in an Ephesians 5 way unless her husband listens to her.

All too often, while she is talking, *you are not listening at all.* Instead you tune her out and don't hear a word she says. Most men are masters of the ancient and proud art of fake listening. We pretend to be listening to our wives when we're not. It looks as if we are listening. All the signs are there: eye contact, leaning forward, nodding the head, a little smile frozen in place. We even give appropriate-sounding responses: "Yeah." "Really?" "That's fine, honey." "Sure." "Great." "That's nice." The truth is, you have no idea what she just said.

It's fun—until she nails you. Face it: you can't fool a woman for long. With an edge to her voice she suddenly says these five horrible words: "Are you listening to me?" Funny how you always hear that phrase. You reply, "Yes, of course I am. I'm right here. I'm looking at you." Then she follows up with those five other words that strike terror in every man's heart: "What did I just say?" Rats. The jig is up. Now you're in real trouble, buddy. The smell of burning rubber fills the room, and you are the one on fire. I can hear the umpire now as he recognizes the truth. You weren't listening to her. Strike one! You lied about it. Strike two. You killed the conversation. Strike three!

When you don't listen to your wife, communication can't take place. That's obvious. You also anger and hurt the woman you love. She thinks you don't care about her because *listening = caring.* If you had any hope that day of her touching you and you touching her in a special way, forget it. When she catches you not listening, she won't say, "Man, I love it when you don't listen to me. It drives me wild. Come over here, Big Boy." Not! You know what is going to happen. You are going to suffer, and it is your own listening-challenged fault.

Listen to your wife. Focus, reflect, and help her feel understood. If you don't listen to her, she won't feel loved. It's one of her most personal and important needs. Learning how to be a good listener is a big part of being a lover.

Listen to Things You Aren't Interested In

Your wife discusses numerous topics that you couldn't care less about. However, this is where marriage demands that you man up. Because you care about her and you want her to know that, you must listen and show interest. Here are two examples of industrial strength listening from my marriage.

My wife, Sandy, is a "crafter." A crafter is a woman who loves crafts. Sandy makes crafts, buys crafts, visits craft stores and craft fairs, and looks through all kinds of craft catalogs. You know what I figured out about crafts? All the craft stores, craft fairs, and craft catalogs sell the same five thousand items. It's the same stuff no matter where you go! Look, when you have seen one stuffed rabbit holding a wooden heart, you have seen them all. And believe me, I have seen them all.

While it is bad enough to get dragged to all the places that sell crafts, Sandy also wants to talk to me about crafts. Does this interest me in even the slightest way? Nope. Do I listen to her? Yes. Why? Because I love her and want to show interest in the things she enjoys. Frankly I wouldn't listen to any other woman on Earth talk about crafts; I would just walk away. For my precious Sandy, I listen. I enter the wonderful world of crafts because that is part of her world. (Plus, I want her to listen to my golf stories.)

My Sandy is also a shopper. Like a lot of women, she enjoys going on shopping trips, especially to clothing stores. I don't mind her taking these trips. What's tough is listening to Sandy's blow-by-blow account of a three-hour shopping trip.

Do you have any idea what it is like listening to this? I'll bet you do. A woman can take five hours to tell you about a three-hour shopping adventure. It's the details—the endless, insufferable, obscure details. I don't want to remember that many inconsequential bits of data. Sandy does and she wants me to hear them.

I could take it if Sandy just showed me what she bought. That would be fine. However, there is a story behind every purchase—and every item *almost* purchased. Then there's a story behind every store she visited. Like the clerk at Walmart who is from Boise, Idaho, and Sandy used to have a friend whose boyfriend moved to Boise and really liked it there. It was sad that they broke up, but he started an organic farm and has done well raising cauliflower. Isn't that interesting? No! But I listen to Sandy's descriptions of her shopping trips because that is what a lover does. When I listen and get involved in these stories, Sandy feels loved. And that is my job: to make her feel loved.

Be an Active Listener

When your wife is talking, what she needs from you is understanding and emotional connection. She is sharing a part of herself with you and hoping you will join her in the experience. When she tells you a story, what she is really saying is: "Honey, this is who I am. Relive this event with me and you'll know me better. And then we'll be closer." The point is not the story itself and the details of what happened. The point is what the story reveals about *her*. That is what she not only wants but also needs you to get about her. She needs you to engage in her world.

In addition to meeting your wife's emotional needs, being an active listener is an important survival skill. When you listen passively to your wife and remain silent, a lot of bad things happen. For starters she will think you aren't listening and will talk more, repeating details over and over, looking for some kind of reaction from you that indicates you are listening *and* understanding. React! You don't want any *more* words, do you?

As her monologue continues, your brain is likely to get overwhelmed and automatically shut down. You will zone out, get distracted, or fall asleep. Of course, she will catch you not paying attention and get upset. Now she is angry and hurt, you're an insensitive jerk who doesn't care about her, and the next few hours (at least) are ruined. You have blown it, and now you'll pay.

Being an active listener will take you from mind-numbing monologues to interesting and need-meeting dialogues with your wife. Here is how you do it.

No distractions

It takes *all your attention* to listen in an active, healthy way. Don't do anything else but listen to her. No TV. No computer. No newspaper or magazine. No children. Your focus is her and what she is saying. You can't even pick your nose and listen to her; you will get distracted. A few minutes into the conversation, when you find what you were looking for up there in your nostril, your wife will realize that she has lost out to a booger!

Set up the best possible environment for active listening. Sit down with your wife every day for thirty minutes in a comfortable, private place at home. This is your talk time. It is your job as her husband and lover to make sure these meetings happen. Shoot for seven days a week. If you miss a couple of days, that is OK; I understand everyone lives hectic lives. Even four or five focused conversations a week would be a huge boost for your marriage.

During these thirty minutes you lower the "Cone of Silence" over your relationship. Without any distractions (you won't even answer the phone or respond to a knock on the door), you will have a good chance to be an active listener. We men are highly distractible creatures, so carving out this "just-the-two-of-us time" is essential.

Reflect and engage

As she talks, look right into her eyes. Feed back to her verbally her key words, phrases, and emotions. A caution: don't repeat everything she says. Just the highlights and how she feels about what she is sharing. This selective repetition of content and identification of emotion is called "reflection." What you are doing is letting her know you understand what she is saying and feeling.

When she is talking and sharing her story, say nothing original. It is all about her. You only open your mouth to repeat and rephrase what *she* is saying and the emotional reaction *she* is having about the experience she is describing. Later in the conversation you can share original thoughts, feelings, and even your famous logic. But not now. In the first part of the conversation the spotlight is on her.

The second active listening skill you need to bring to the conversation is engagement. Engage your wife by reacting emotionally as she speaks. When you reflect, you build understanding. When you engage, you connect with her on an emotional level. To engage is to walk in her shoes and try to feel what she is feeling. As she tells her story, you are reliving the experience with her.

Ask her questions about what she is describing. Work to mirror her emotions. If she is angry, you get angry. If she is happy, reflect that joyful mood. If she expresses sadness and is kind of depressed, you feel these emotions as well. No one, especially the husband, is perfect at this engagement process. Just do your best. Believe me, she will appreciate it. When she compares notes with her girlfriends (which she likely will), you will come out smelling like a rose.

How am I doing?

To learn these active listening skills, you need your wife to evaluate your progress. During these conversations ask her how you're doing as a listener:

- "Do you think I'm getting it?"

- "Do you feel understood?"

- "Do you feel connected to me?"

Asking these questions will impress her and make her feel closer to you. The feedback she gives you will help you dramatically improve your listening skills. You can make corrections in the same conversation and get back on track. If she tells you that you have missed some content or you aren't reacting with enough emotion, ask her to go over that part of the story again. That won't bother her in the least! In fact, she will enjoy going over it again.

Let her teach you how to listen with reflection and engagement. She is a master of conversational skills—she has been doing it her whole life. Swallow your male pride and allow her to guide you in the active listening process. No one else has to know. This can be a secret between the two of you. When you listen actively, your wife will talk less. That's a good thing. She'll feel understood and loved, and your talks will become much more interesting, stimulating, and revealing. And that leads to intimacy. You will get drawn into the conversation and get warmed up. That will help you open up and talk when your turn comes.

Listen When There Is Conflict

If you want to be a lover, you have to listen closely to your wife when she is saying something difficult to hear. Criticism. Anger. Hurt. Intense negative emotion. Oh, boy. This is beyond tough. You know the drill. She is walking down the hallway and she's coming for you. She has that *look.* You glance behind you, but the door is too far away. You're trapped—trapped like a dog.

If you are like me, you will have to fight getting defensive, growing angry and firing back at her, or ignoring her and walking away. I hate conflict with Sandy. Absolutely hate it. I will do anything to get out of it, particularly if I think I am being unjustly accused. (Of course, I always think I'm being unjustly accused.)

It is especially important to be an active listener when you are in a conflict with your woman and her emotional intensity spikes. If you do anything else, you are wrong.

- If you use logic and patiently explain how what she is saying doesn't make a whole lot of sense, you're an unfeeling cad...and you are wrong.

- If you raise your voice just a little and express your position, you are mean, have hurt her feelings...and you are wrong.

- If you listen but don't say anything, you are not paying attention to her and don't care about what she's saying...and you are wrong.

- If you tell her this really isn't a good time to be discussing this (the last two minutes of the national championship, you have a huge work meeting in twenty minutes, or it's midnight and you are flat on your back in bed and very drowsy...), you are a selfish bozo, she won't likely talk to you any time soon...and you are wrong.

Get the picture? When your woman is upset, let her talk and say nothing original until she has fully expressed herself and feels understood. Never interrupt a woman when she is on a roll—unless you want to suffer. As she points her finger and emotes all over the room, your job is to reflect and engage. You had better get comfortable because when a woman is upset, she talks twice as long.

It takes a real man, a courageous lover, to stand in the hurricane and be an active listener. But if you can pull this off, she will feel understood and calm down. Then you can give your view of the situation, and she will be able to listen. Keep in mind, it is always one at a time in a conflict conversation. One partner *speaks* and the other actively *listens*.

Talk to Her

Listening is crucial, but it is not enough to meet your wife's emotional needs. To be an Ephesians 5:25 husband, you also have to *talk* to her—and I don't mean safe, superficial topics. Reporting facts about your job, current events, finances, the kids, or sports won't do her or your relationship any good. She can talk to the lawn man about these topics. I mean deeper, personal stuff. What do you think and feel *inside* about the events of your day? What are you worried about? How do you feel about your relationship with her, the kids, and close friends? What are your hopes and dreams? How is your walk with Christ? These are the topics your wife desperately wants you to share with her.

You may say, "Dave, I'm just not a talker." That is a big, fat cop-out. I know because I used that line for years with Sandy. What you are telling her with that kind of excuse is, "I'm choosing not to meet one of your most important needs, even if it makes you feel unhappy and unloved for the rest of our marriage." Now, if you are single, you don't have to talk on such a personal level with a woman. That is fine—if you're single. But you're not. *You* married this woman and now *you* have to learn to talk to her.

You will never talk as much as she does. Don't worry. You will never have her volume of words or emotional intensity. Still, you can work your way to the place where you talk enough to make her feel loved and close to you.

How to start? Try this. Prepare for your daily talk with your wife by carrying around a small notepad, which you can find in any drugstore. As you go through your day and things happen that you think might interest your wife, jot them down. It might be something that made you feel angry, frustrated, or happy, or an interesting interaction with another person. It might be something God showed you in Scripture or private prayer time. Then, during your one-on-one time, you will have a list of things to share. Don't trust your memory: you don't have one! Use the pad.

Understand and Respect Her

In 1 Peter 3:7, God delivers a devastating message to husbands:

> You husbands in the same way, live with your wives in an understanding way, as with someone weaker, since she is a woman; and show her honor as a fellow heir of the grace of life, so that your prayers will not be hindered.

Read that last clause again carefully. If you don't demonstrate understanding, consideration, and honor to your spouse, your prayers will be blocked! Your relationship with your heavenly Father will be limited. I am convinced this is the reason many husbands are spiritually dry. You can't treat your wife poorly and expect closeness with God. That is what this verse says. Caring for your precious wife with understanding and respect is of paramount importance for God. It is so important that if you fail to do this, your communication with Him will dry up. That is the worst possible consequence.

The picture Peter painted here is of someone handling a delicate, fragile work of art of great value such as the *Mona Lisa*, the most famous painting in the world that hangs in The Louvre Museum in Paris, France.

What if I met you at one of my marriage seminars and handed you the *Mona Lisa*? I wonder: How you would handle it? With extreme care. You wouldn't want to be known as the guy who dropped the *Mona Lisa* and broke it. Your wife has infinitely more value than a mere painting. God wants you—He orders you—to handle her softly and gently.

One way to obey this verse is to lower your voice when you are angry. Don't act as if you are arguing with a buddy about politics or your favorite sports team. A loud voice and a harsh tone crush a woman's spirit. Have you ever had this happen to you? Your wife is angry and raising her voice. She sounds mean and strong. But when you fire back one—just one—statement in a loud voice, she dissolves into tears. Suddenly you are the bad guy! This is because she is a very sensitive being and can't tolerate harsh treatment. Keep your voice down. If you have an anger problem, get professional help to fix it.

Another way to be a 1 Peter 3:7 husband is to say, "I'm sorry," when you blow it. Many husbands can't seem to say these words. If your wife feels hurt or upset, you had better be sorry and you better say it. If she leaves the room in the midst of an argument, wait a few minutes. Then go after her. She may say, "Don't bother following me." Follow her anyway—that is what she wants. Say, "I'm sorry, honey," and mean it. It has to be heartfelt to convince her. Keep saying it until she feels better. If she has been hurt, she needs your reassurance.

Finally, you can communicate understanding and respect by asking for her evaluation of you as a husband on a monthly basis. This takes guts, but it's what a lover does. Ask her how you're doing as a husband. Don't assume you're doing a good job. Ask her. She is the only one who knows. Take her evaluation seriously and make whatever adjustments she suggests. She will feel loved and honored. Not only will she smile, but also so will God.

Chapter 7

God Says:
Be a Romancer and a Leader

FOR A WOMAN there is no real love without romance. In nearly twenty-five years as a clinical psychologist and seminar leader I have not seen a single exception to this rule. Not one. Your wife needs you to romance her regularly. If you fail to be a romancer, she will feel unloved and have an ache in her heart that will not go away.

Most men are romantic only during courtship. We're not stupid. We realize what it takes to get her to say "yes" to our marriage proposal. When we're pursuing her, we are romantic as all get out. Wining and dining and flowering and candying and talking. Yes, even talking! We are not going to talk after we get married, but she doesn't have to know that.

When we have bagged her, like every great hunter we put her up on the wall in the den and find new fields to conquer. The pressure is off. Mission accomplished! We were Sir Lancelot, her dashing romantic hero on the white horse. Now we're a slug, her boring intimacy avoider, wearing a hole in the recliner.

Listen, husbands, when you stop the romance, she assumes you don't love her anymore. And she is absolutely right! You can't convince her otherwise because she must be romanced to feel loved. You say, "I'm just not a romantic guy." I say, "Fine. *Get over it.* Your wife needs romance!"

God Loves Romance!

The fact that your wife needs to be romanced didn't originate with me. This is God's idea. He created woman, and He makes it clear she needs her husband to romance her. God loves romance. He wants it to be an integral part of every marriage. There is even a whole book in the Bible devoted to romance, love, and sex: Song of Solomon. You have likely heard about *Reader's Digest* condensed version of popular books. Well, here is the Dave Clarke condensed version of the Song of Solomon:

- Boy meets girl.

- Boy and girl fall in love.

- Boy is very romantic as he courts girl.

- Boy and girl get married.

- Boy continues to romance girl for the rest of their married life.

- Girl is happy, boy is happy, and their marriage is terrific.

- God is pleased and blesses them.

The boy is King Solomon. The girl is Shulamith. The Song of Solomon is the story of their courtship and marriage. The joy, passion, and fulfillment they experienced literally leap off the pages of this book. God wants their story to be your story. And it can be, if you learn how to romance your wife and then put those plans into action. That is what the Song of Solomon is all about; it is the secret to the powerful, enduring love between Solomon and his wife.

The Power of Verbal Romance

Read Song of Solomon 2:8–9, and you'll get a clear picture of how Shulamith felt about her man, Solomon:

> Listen! My beloved! Behold, he is coming, climbing on the mountains, leaping on the hills! My beloved is like a gazelle or a young stag. Behold, he is standing behind our wall, he is looking through the windows, he is peering through the lattice.

Shulamith is at home; Solomon has been out doing whatever kings do. With Solomon about to return home, these verses describe his wife's anticipation. As he draws closer and closer, she is so excited she can barely contain herself. She even calls him a "young stag." When was the last time your wife called you a young stag? (Yeah, thought so.) Does she tremble with excitement when she hears your car in the driveway? Does her heart flutter with passion as she rushes up to greet you? Probably not. You are lucky if she says, "Hi, honey" and gives you a token peck on the cheek.

Why? Why can't Shulamith wait to see her man? Why does she go into spasms of joy when she knows he is about to come in the door? The answer appears in the first six verses of chapter 4. Here are some excerpts from this passage.

> How beautiful you are, my darling, how beautiful you are! Your eyes are like doves behind your veil; your hair is like a flock of goats that have descended from Mount Gilead. Your teeth are like a flock of newly shorn ewes.... Your lips are like a scarlet thread, and your mouth is lovely. Your temples are like a slice of a pomegranate.... Your neck is like the tower of David.... Your two breasts are like two fawns.

Do you get it? Solomon romanced his lady! He treated her like a queen! He showered her with romantic word pictures of how gorgeous she was! That is why she loved him so much and looked forward to seeing him. She couldn't wait to return his love.

If you want your woman to respond with the same kind of passion and intensity, you need to verbally romance her. Tell her often that she is beautiful!

Now, some cultural context: please don't try Solomon's descriptions today. A husband called me after he and his wife attended one of my marriage seminars to say, "Dave, your Song of Solomon romantic idea didn't work for me." I asked, "What do you mean?" He responded, "The other day my wife and I were coming out of church. I told her that the sunlight made her hair look like a flock of goats. She was insulted!" I replied, "You dummy! Those lines worked only back in those days. You need to come up with some contemporary romantic descriptions." (You just can't help some people.)

Instead imitate Solomon's habit of verbalizing his love on a regular basis. He didn't use a quick, "Love ya, honey;" he went overboard. Solomon is our role model. You may say, "I'm just not an expressive guy." I say, "Fine. Get over it! Just like Shulamith, your wife needs to hear how beautiful she is, over and over and over."

Your wife is the most beautiful woman in the world, right? Well then, tell her. Compliment her physical beauty, her emotional beauty, and her spiritual beauty. Do it out loud, right to her face. Do it often. A woman never gets tired of this. Shulamith never said, "Oh, Solomon, stop! You're embarrassing me with all these compliments." She just drank in his verbal praise. Romance filled her heart with love, and she loved him right back.

I am not asking you to be like Solomon twenty-four hours a day. Frankly no one has that kind of stamina. Just romance your wife regularly and see what happens. She will feel loved! And that is your job: to make sure she feels loved. And you will be loved in return. You want your wife to be warm, soft, and attentive to your needs, don't you? You want her to be more interested in sex and more passionate and responsive in the bedroom? Of course! That's what all husbands want. Then romance her. It will be returned to you a hundred times over!

Create a Little Romance

To help get you started, here are some behaviors that your wife *and* you will find romantic:

One date a week

I strongly recommend you take your woman out on a date once a week. Just the two of you. No children. That is what baby-sitters are for. In fact, you be the one to call a babysitter and sign her up. Make sure you have a list of three or four teenage girls. Once they get a social life (i.e., a boyfriend), it's often the kiss of death. If you can get family to watch your kids for free, fine. Or maybe you can babysit another couple's kids one night, and they can babysit yours the next.

Early in the week look into your wife's lovely eyes and ask, "Would you like to go out with me this Saturday night?" I say Saturday because that is my date night with Sandy. Women like to be asked. Sandy and I go out every Saturday night, but I still ask her every Monday or Tuesday. She doesn't say, "Why are you asking me? I know we're going out Saturday. We always do." Oh, no. My queen smiles and says, "Yes, Dave. I would love to go out on Saturday."

Don't make your wife always come up with plans. You have a brain, don't you? At least every other week you decide the plan for the date. Be creative. Plan something you think she would enjoy.

A walk in the evening

Taking a walk together around your neighborhood in the evening can be very romantic. Do this two or three times a week. It's low-key, relaxing, and fun. Just make sure you hold her hand;

physical contact is what creates the romantic mood. You are not walking with your mother, your aunt, or your sister. You are walking with your sweetheart! If your wife has a steel hook for a hand, hold the hook. It may be a little cold in the winter, but go ahead.

Sometimes husbands whine to me, "Oh, but it's too hot to walk!"

I tell these babies, "I know it's hot. That's the beauty of it. Walk with her and get all sweaty. Then take a shower together. It's not about the walk, you dummy. It's about the shower."

A small gift

About once a month buy your wife an inexpensive little something. She will absolutely love the fact that you thought about her. It isn't the gift but the love and thoughtfulness it symbolizes that she will appreciate. Remember: don't give this gift to her in a plastic grocery bag or a plain brown wrapper! This isn't dog food or groceries. Have someone at the store wrap it, or wrap it yourself.

A romantic card

Once about every two weeks get your dear wife a greeting card with a romantic message. This card must be gushy, mushy, and sentimental. Not "be my friend," but, "Your stunning beauty and sweet spirit bring color and life into my dark and lonely world." Or, "You are my perfect mate and satisfy the deepest longings of my heart." You get the idea.

Be creative with the way you present her with the card too. Try leaving it on her pillow in your bedroom one time and at the dinner table the next. Then mail it to her. Put it on her car seat. Use your imagination. Please, please, please, don't just sign your name. Your woman wants to read a paragraph from you about how much you love her and why. You don't have to be Shakespeare. No one is going to publish your little love notes. Compliment her and thank her for being who she is. Write from your heart. She will love it and love you for doing it.

Ask her what she finds romantic

While most wives will feel loved and romanced with these four behaviors, they are just the tip of the romantic iceberg. Your wife needs to be romanced in a variety of ways. To make sure you are acting like her Sir Lancelot, ask her once every two months what she finds romantic. She thinks about romance all the time. She gets ideas about romance from her friends, books and magazines, and her own imagination. So she will likely offer a list of romantic ideas every time you ask. Write them down, follow through, do them, and you will be her romantic hero.

Touching without intercourse

Read that heading again: touching without intercourse. Do you have any idea what this is? Like most men, I didn't always know. However, after years of research, I have made a stunning discovery—I should win the Nobel Prize in science for my breakthrough. I hope you are sitting down. Here it is: it is possible to touch a female *without* moving on to intercourse. Now I have only tested this on laboratory rats, but they are doing quite well. So I just know you human husbands can manage.

Touch your wife. Kiss her. Rub her neck. Make out with her and…that's all. *Don't ask for intercourse.* Can you picture this? She will be so shocked, she may say, "Honey, don't you want something else?" That is your cue to say, "No, sweetheart, I'm just loving you for you." You won't mean it, but you'll say it. Now the important part: stick with it!

Obviously there are times when you both will want to move on to the next level. God wants intercourse to be a regular part of every married couple's life together, but not every time you touch her! If every time you lay a hand on her you push for intercourse, she will feel used and cheap. Ask your wife if that is true. She will tell you that Dr. Clarke is, once again, correct. Of course I am correct. I am an expert. Actually I learned this truth the hard way from my wife.

However, if your spouse insists on intercourse and begs you for it, go ahead. If that is her need, it is your sworn duty as her husband to meet it. As you frequently romance your queen and touch her without expecting intercourse, there may come a time when she says, "Young stag, take me! Take me now!"

Romance her when you don't have to

Don't romance your wife only on special occasions such as her birthday, Valentine's Day, and your anniversary. Almost every dimwit husband in the world does that! God help you if you fail to come through on these dates! Romance her for no reason other than you love her. That is what it's all about. You don't do it because you have to or because she expects it. You do it because you love her. You want her to know that and to feel that.

Whatever you do, don't start romance and then stop. This crushes a woman. It is better not to start at all than to start and then stop. All you have to do is keep up a steady stream of romance until you die. When you're dead, I will let you off the hook. Your last words in the hospital, as you squeeze her hand, ought to be: "Well, I guess we're not going out on our date this weekend." And then you're gone, leaving a legacy as a man who loved his woman and romanced her to the end.

Be a Leader

Finally, God says: be a leader.

> Wives, be subject to your own husbands, as to the Lord. For the husband is the head of the wife, as Christ also is the head of the church, He Himself being the Savior of the body. But as the church is subject to Christ, so also the wives ought to be to their husbands in everything.
> —Ephesians 5:22–24

That is a pretty clear message, isn't it? Headship equals leadership. God gave us, as husbands, the job of leader in the marriage relationship and in the home. More husbands fail in this area than in almost any other. Why? Because being a leader is difficult. How do we figure out the right way to lead our wives? By looking at Jesus. As in every area of life we need to follow the example Christ set when He walked the earth. Here are some ideas.

Lead as Christ led

To be a biblical leader we must lead as Christ led. In Matthew 20:25–28 Jesus summed up His leadership style:

> You know that the rulers of the Gentiles lord it over them, and their great men exercise authority over them. It is not this way among you, but whoever wishes to become great among you shall be your servant, and whoever wishes to be first among you shall be your slave; just as the Son of Man did not come to be served, but to serve, and to give His life a ransom for many.

One of the most powerful illustrations of Christ's commitment to lead by serving appears in John 13:3–5. Read this passage and try to picture in your mind what Jesus is doing.

> Jesus, knowing that the Father had given all things into His hands, and that He had come forth from God and was going back to God, got up from supper, and laid aside His garments and taking a towel, He girded Himself. Then He poured water into the basin, and began to wash the disciples' feet and to wipe them with the towel with which He was girded.

Can you imagine this scene? Jesus Christ is washing the disciples' dirty, dust-covered feet. And these men walked everywhere! This is the King of the universe washing smelly, dust-covered feet that likely stunk worse than your gym bag after you stow it in the corner of your closet for a month! Why? Because that is what a leader does.

The bottom line is this: Christ, God and Savior, was (and is) a servant-leader, one who leads by identifying the needs of others and meeting them. Husbands are to be servant-leaders, leading their wives by serving them.

If you lead by serving, your woman will follow you anywhere. If you serve your wife faithfully by meeting her needs, it makes it easier for her to submit to you. It makes it easier for her to support you in a decision with which she disagrees. It makes it easier for her to love and respect you. And it makes it easier for her to meet your needs.

Here are four practical ways you can be a servant-leader:

Method one: Do your share of household chores

Don't do only the bare minimum. Do *more* than you have to do! This is the most obvious way to be a servant-leader. Can you imagine Jesus living in a home and not lifting a finger? Sitting on the couch all day? Avoiding jobs whenever possible? No way! I know, you think you have your wife's welfare in mind when you don't do much around the house. After all, you are trying to prepare her for widowhood. Right! In truth you are just being selfish and lazy. I know, because that is how I used to be.

Just like my wife, Sandy, your wife wants to be part of a team. The condition of her house is extremely important to a woman, and she needs your help to keep it clean and in order. Ask your wife every day what chores need to be done. Do your part by completing regular jobs faithfully *and* asking her about extra ways you can be of service. She will feel closer to you. She will follow you. She will also devote more time and energy to you.

Method two: Meet her needs

If you fail to meet your wife's needs, you are not fulfilling your responsibilities as a servant-leader. Remember, it is not your duty to meet *all* of her needs, just the needs a husband can meet. Unlike Jesus, you don't know what her needs are; don't assume you automatically know. You will be wrong. The *only* way to find out is to ask her daily—more than once—about needs. Your wife is an emotional, unpredictable creature, and so her needs will change throughout the day. Ask her in the morning before you go to work. Call her at lunchtime and ask her. When you get home from work, ask her again.

Make it clear to her that you are not just willing to do chores. You want to know about her physical, emotional, and spiritual needs—the whole enchilada. Just asking communicates love and concern, but following through is even better. So don't ask unless you intend to do something. Do what I do when I ask Sandy what her needs are: to make certain I don't forget, I jot them down on my pad so I won't disappoint her.

Method three: Include her in decisions

Always, always, always ask your wife for input before any significant decision. If you are not sure of its significance, then ask. It is demeaning, insulting, and a failure in servant leadership to make any important decision without first consulting her. To put the shoe on the other foot, how would you feel if she went out and bought a family sedan without even telling you she planned to do it? You need to consider her viewpoint, wisdom, and intuition. After all, she is your equal partner in this relationship, not someone you can boss around as king! Besides, how can you expect her to support you in a decision that she has no part in making?

Involve her in household finances. She needs to know where every penny is going. Make financial decisions together: major purchases, developing a budget, investments, and tithing all require her input. Whether she has an accounting degree or relies on you to pay bills, balance the checking account, and manage the credit and debit card statements is irrelevant. I know husbands who tell their wives absolutely nothing about their financial situation. Why? Is this top secret information? Are you in the CIA? Tell her! Keep her involved.

Method four: Be her champion

Your woman is more than your wife and a mother. She is a person with her own gifts, abilities, hopes, and dreams. Every wife needs to develop her own life *outside the home*. She needs her own identity, activities, and unique way of impacting the world for Christ. She loves being a wife and a mom, but she needs more.

One of your jobs as a servant-leader is to be her champion as she branches out and fulfills her dreams as an independent person. Ask her what she wants to do with other facets of her life. It may be time with her girlfriends, more education, a job outside the home, service in the church, a hobby, or a combination of all these. When she tells you what she needs, do everything you can to help her. She has gone to great lengths for you and the kids, hasn't she? Now it is her turn.

Caution: Don't let your imagination run wild here. She won't go crazy and leave you and the kids in the lurch. She won't run off to Hawaii to follow her dream of surfing the Banzai Pipeline. She will still be a great wife and mother. But she will also be joyful, content, confident, and energized as a person. And appreciative of the man who encouraged her and helped her spread her wings.

A Final Challenge

I know you love your wife. Now you must learn to love her the way she needs to be loved. The way I have described in these last three chapters. The way God says to love her: be a godly man, be a lover, be a romancer, and be a leader.

Whew! It is a lot to take in, isn't it? It is not going to be easy to carry out these four roles. You need help to do it. That is why I wrote this book. You can read the rest of it if you want. That would certainly be helpful for you, but you don't have to. Your wife has and will be asking you to do certain behaviors. If you want to become the husband she needs you to be, you will decide to work with her and do what she asks. It will be good for her. It will be good for you. It will be very good for your marriage. So don't resist. Cooperate and your life together will blossom.

STEP THREE

HONEY, I NEED TO FORGIVE YOU

Chapter 8

Smiling on the Outside, Dying on the Inside

T HE WIFE AND husband settled in on my couch for our first joint therapy session. In their mid- to late thirties, they had been married almost fifteen years and had two children. Both professed to know Christ personally and were actively involved in a Bible-teaching church. However, when I asked them why they had come to see me, it became clear very quickly that they had the classic "married...but lonely" marriage.

The husband told me I would have to find out from his wife why they were there, because he didn't have a clue. I thought to myself, "You're right, Buddy. You don't have a clue." I knew exactly what he was going to say next. I could have mouthed the words right along with him. He gave me the same speech that hundreds of intimacy avoiders have delivered in my office. Here it is, with my editorial comments—things I thought but did not say out loud—added:

He Just Doesn't Get It

Husband: I'm happy in our marriage.

Me: Well, that's great for you. Isn't there someone else involved?

Husband: We're doing fine.

Me: If you say so, then it must be true.

Husband: We have a good life. We make a good income and have a nice home, good investments, two vacations a year, great friends, two super kids, a terrific church, and good health.

Me: Ah, the American dream! Guess what? A good life doesn't equal a good marriage. Funny thing—you didn't mention love, passion, or intimacy.

Husband: I'm a good husband. I don't drink, go to bars, do drugs, beat her, or have affairs. I work hard, provide for my family, go to church, and take care of the yard and the cars.

Me: No one is questioning your character. I will acknowledge that you're a good guy, not a monster. But being a good husband requires communication skills, romance, and spiritual leadership. God doesn't say, "Don't be a monster." God says, "Love your wives, just as Christ also loved the church" (Eph. 5:25).

Husband: I'm not the most romantic guy in the world.

Me: Translation: I'm about the least romantic guy in the world.

Husband: We have a good sex life.

Me: Translation: "I get sex when I want it." Sex might be good for you, but I doubt it's good for her.

Husband: My wife is a good woman. She takes care of all my needs. She cleans the house, does the laundry, cooks the meals, and takes care of the kids.

Me: It sounds as though you're describing Betty Crocker or Martha Stewart. Or *your mother*. And it's still all about you. How about your wife and her needs? What do you do for her?

Husband: We're older now. So our love isn't the passionate, intense kind we had back when we first got together. Still, it is a solid, committed, and comfortable love.

Me: What are you, ninety years old? It sounds as though you're talking about an old shoe. Commitment is good, but commitment plus romance, excitement, and emotional closeness is much better. That's what God desires for you both.

Husband: I love my wife.

Me: No, you don't. Not by God's definition. And not by hers either. Love is something you *do*.

Husband: We don't have any marriage problems. We don't need a psychologist.

I did speak after this last comment. I almost said, "Mr. Intimacy Avoider, if you have no marriage problems, what are you doing here in my office?" Fortunately, with great effort, I bit my tongue and instead said, "OK, thanks for sharing. That's *your* view, and I understand how you see things. Now let's hear from your wife."

She Didn't Help Him Get It

As she prepared to talk, the wife looked uncomfortable. She fidgeted, smoothed her dress out a few times, and shot nervous glances at her husband and me. I knew—just knew—that she was going to deliver the standard, "I'll nibble around the edges and ask for changes without causing him to be angry or hurt" wimpy state-of-the-marriage address. And that is exactly what she did. Below are her words, accompanied by my unspoken thoughts:

Wife: Honey, I want you to know first of all that you are a really good husband.

Me: No, he's not! The man's an IA! Please, I'm begging you, don't list all of his good points as a husband.

Wife: It would be hard to list all your good points as a husband, but let me try. You work hard, you provide the money we need to live, you're a great dad, you help around the house, you don't drink or do other sinful behaviors that would harm me and the kids, you take care of the cars, you keep the yard looking beautiful...

Me: I think I'm going to throw up. You are dying inside because you have no emotional connection to this man, but at least when you look out the window the yard is gorgeous. I bet you wouldn't mind having the most scraggly, weed-infested yard in the neighborhood if you could just have two or three deep, personal conversations a week with your husband.

Wife: I love you, honey. And I know you love me. We have a good life together.

Me: Stop calling him honey! Don't say you love him and that he loves you. That is not what he needs to hear. You are being way too nice!

Wife: But there are a few things in our marriage I want to see improve. Over the last few years especially I just haven't felt like we...

Me: Too late. Don't bother. You took too long getting to the *but* part. Your husband is not going to listen to your real concerns. Why should he? You just spent five minutes complimenting him and confirming what he already believes: that he is a good husband, the two of you still love each other, you have a good life together, and what in the world are we doing in this shrink's office? If you were a boss and were telling an employee how to improve his job performance, maybe you would begin by listing his good points. This is a *very* different situation.

Just as she tentatively tiptoed into telling her husband about the weak areas of their marriage, he glanced at me with a little smirk on his face. His look said it all: "See, Doc, what did I tell you? You heard her. We're OK. She may have a few minor beefs, but our marriage is strong; it is fine. Doggone it, I'm a good husband."

With her husband only half-listening, she finally shared what she thought was wrong with their marriage:

> Our main problem is communication. We only talk about superficial, mundane things: home improvements, our jobs, the kids' activities and schedules, and what our parents are doing. We don't sit down together and really talk. He doesn't open up and share on a personal level. I want to know who he is and what he's thinking and feeling inside. I love him. I'm glad I married him. He's good to me. But I don't *know* him. I want intimate, deep conversations that will lead to real closeness. We get along, but I want more than that. I don't know, maybe I'm asking for too much. None of my girlfriends have this kind of emotional connection with their husbands either.
>
> I would also like us to learn how to work through conflicts. Honey, please don't clam up and walk away when we have something difficult or painful to discuss. When you do, it leaves me hanging. I want to talk out my feelings and reach some kind of a resolution. When you refuse to face

the conflict, all my emotions get bottled up inside and that hurts me. Plus, we can't work out any solution or compromise. Life just goes on. I think you forget about the issue, but I don't.

At this point in the session, I sensed that this lady harbored an Olympic-sized pool of smoldering resentments. I could feel the anger percolating in her like my morning coffee. I tried to tap it by asking, "It makes you really angry when he won't deal with a conflict, doesn't it?" She responded, a little too quickly, "Oh, no. Not angry. Just hurt and a little disappointed."

I thought to myself, "Baloney. You're angry all right. It's buried deep, but it's there." So I tried again (out loud): "I think all the missed opportunities for conversation, the lack of emotional intimacy, and his refusal to allow you to express yourself in conflicts have created resentments inside you. I don't think you want these resentments, but I think you have them."

She looked shocked and stammered back, "No! No, no, no. I don't resent my husband. I do get hurt and frustrated when we don't talk personally or deal with a conflict, but those feelings go away. I think you're misunderstanding me. Our marriage is good. I just want it to be better."

I could have said, "Stop saying your marriage is good. Every time you say that, you reinforce your husband's belief that you don't need therapy, that you are happy with him, and that your marriage doesn't require any changes. The case you just gave for improving your marriage is weak and didn't even get close to getting your husband's attention.

"Your comments were way too general. Way too nice and sweet. There was no punch. No urgency. No emotion. I got the impression you were talking about someone else's marriage that could stand just a little improvement. This is *your* marriage, and you're not paying me your hard-earned money to tell me you're doing well and just want a few changes. You're smiling on the outside and dying on the inside.

"When your husband won't meet your important, God-given needs, it hurts you and angers you. Every single time. And when you aren't even allowed to vent those feelings, they turn into resentment. You're still able to stuff these resentments down deep. You're not even aware you have them. But they're there, and if I can't get you to tap into them and express them directly with your husband, they will eventually destroy your respect and love for him. It's already happening, and you don't even realize it."

I could have said these things, but I didn't. At least not right then. The therapy hour was up, and it wouldn't have done any good anyway. This wife was not ready to admit that her marriage was lousy and that she was hanging on to some heavy-duty resentments against her husband. I went to plan B and scheduled individual therapy sessions with each of them for the following week. Sometimes I can get through to a spouse when I see him or her alone.

"She'll Get Over It, Doc"

I had forty-five minutes to convince this husband that his marriage was in serious trouble and changes were necessary. As he sat down, I said, "I want you to listen to me for the next fifteen minutes. Listen closely. You have a serious problem on your hands. I'm taking the gloves off, and I'm going to give it to you straight." Here's a brief summary of the points I hammered home:

- "This is your second session in a Christian psychologist's office. Your wife asked you to come to therapy. There is no way she would do that unless she was very concerned about your marriage. That is serious."

- "You are an intimacy avoider. Like many husbands, you keep all your feelings and thoughts locked away inside. You don't talk personally with your wife. You don't share with her what's going on in your life, career, spiritual walk with God, relationship with her, or your hopes and dreams. That is serious."

- "From the history I took of your childhood in our first session, I know why you're an intimacy avoider. Your father is an intimacy avoider. He taught you how to clam up and stuff everything personal way down deep. Your mom put up with it, so naturally you expect your wife to put up with it. That is serious."

- "You are not obeying God's instructions for a husband. You are not loving her the Ephesians 5:25 way, which is loving her the way Christ loved the church. You are not loving her the 1 Peter 3:7 way, which is treating her gently and tenderly meeting her needs. You are not loving her the Song of Solomon way, which is loving her with passion and romance. You are not loving her the Ephesians 5:23–24 and John 13:3–5 way, which is leading her by serving her. You are loving her your way, not God's way. That is serious."

- "I know from our first session that your sex life isn't full of passion, excitement, or intimacy. In fact, it is boring and routine. I'm telling you frankly, that is *your* fault. Your wife cannot respond sexually unless she is emotionally connected to you. Your sex life is pretty poor, isn't it? How about no sex at all? That is in your future if you don't become a better husband. That is serious."

- "Your wife's number-one need is to feel close to you. She wants and needs to experience life *together*, not as two separate persons. To have the Genesis 2:24 one-flesh relationship God desires for every married couple, you must learn to open up and share personally. As long as you're an intimacy avoider, you won't meet this critical, God-given need in her life. That is serious."

- "Over the years you have hurt your wife repeatedly. I know you haven't meant to, but you have. Every time you clammed up and chose to not share personally, you hurt her. Every time you avoided talking through a conflict, you hurt her. Every time you failed to romance her, you hurt her. All those hurts are still there, inside of her. They have turned into resentments and are eating away at her love for you. If she doesn't express them soon, she will hit the wall and have no feelings for you at all. That is *really* serious."

After firing these verbal bullets, I sat back and waited for his angry, defensive, and rationalization-filled response. I wasn't disappointed. He quickly told me he disagreed and said the terrible picture I had painted of his marriage wasn't even close to the truth. "Look, things aren't that serious," he said, shrugging. "I know I can be a better husband, but I'm doing a good job. Nobody's perfect. She's a little upset now, but it'll pass. I know my woman. She'll get over it, Doc. She always does."

And then he added the real kicker, the statement that revealed why he thought his marriage was fine: "Doc, you're saying we're in serious trouble, but *she's* not saying that. You heard her in that first session. She's not angry. She's not letting me have it. She may want some improvements, but she's not telling me she resents me."

"I know she's not letting you have it," I replied. "But believe me, she has big-time resentments against you. She's stuffing them and faking it with you. Like most good wives, she finds it very difficult to express anger, deep hurt, and resentments with you. One day, though, she will be through faking and will turn completely away from you. Her resentments will drive her to give up on you and move on rather than just live in a cold, emotionless, romanceless cell. You have a small window of opportunity to act and stop her from writing you off. So you had better get to work."

I urged him to quickly do three things:

1. Call his mother and have a heart-to-heart talk about what it was really like living with his dad, the original IA.

2. Work to change as a husband and love his wife the way *she* needed to be loved.

3. Encourage—push if necessary—his wife to express directly all her resentments.

He refused all three action steps. He just couldn't see what all the fuss was about: "I know you mean well, Doc, but all this psychobabble isn't for us. When you see her in her session tomorrow, I'm sure you'll realize that she's not all that upset."

Good Wives Don't Get Angry, Do They?

Well, so far I had batted zero for one. Now I had forty-five minutes to convince his wife that it was essential to get in touch with her resentments and express them directly to her husband. I knew something she didn't: her marriage was at stake. So I went after her hammer and tongs with these arguments:

- "You are filled with anger and hurt. All of your husband's intimacy avoider behaviors have created a vast pool of inner resentments. Don't tell me he is a good husband. He is a lousy husband! Don't tell me you've forgiven him for not meeting your most important needs. You haven't! To forgive, you first must express the pain directly to the one who caused it."

- "If you don't get your resentments out, even if he genuinely changed, it wouldn't make any difference to you. It wouldn't be enough because the resentments would outweigh his improvements. Every mistake he made would energize the resentment pool."

- "I wouldn't worry about him changing. If you don't tell him your resentments, he won't realize how serious things are. He will keep thinking what he is thinking now—that your marriage is fine and dandy. So he won't change. He has no reason to do anything differently! That is your fault."

- "Your unexpressed resentments will limit your ability to be a good wife. You will be irritable and impatient with him, you won't be supportive and encouraging, you won't be a responsive sexual partner, you will overreact and be nastier in conflicts, and you won't meet his needs."

- "Worst of all, it is likely your resentments will kill your feelings of respect and love. The day will come when you are completely numb toward him. You won't care; you will just want out of the marriage. Don't look so shocked. It's already happening. You haven't hit the wall yet, but you're awfully close."

She admitted that she did have some "anger, hurt, and resentment" because of her husband not meeting her needs. Then she added, "It isn't that much, and I don't want to express these feelings to him." Here are her four reasons and my responses:

Wife: Expressing anger and resentments just isn't Christian.

Me: No, it *is* Christian. The Bible teaches us to "speak the truth in love" (Eph. 4:15, NLT), to "be angry, and yet do not sin" (Eph. 4:26), and to deal directly with anyone with whom we have an unresolved issue (Matt. 5:23–24).

Wife: But telling him how I really feel wouldn't be submissive.

Me: Quite the opposite. A big part of being submissive is being honest with your husband. Your job is to help him lead. How can he be an effective leader if he doesn't know what you need? Plus, your buried resentments will cause you to undermine his authority.

Wife: I'm scared of my anger. If you're right, and it's pretty intense, I don't know if I can handle it. I don't like being angry. I was raised not to be angry, because it leads to damaged relationships.

Me: OK, now we're getting to the real reasons. It will be difficult and scary to express your internalized anger. But you can do it, and you will not drop dead or turn into a crazy woman. You will clean it out and feel much better. You need to be much more scared of the anger you don't express. It will do tremendous damage to you, your husband, and your marriage.

Wife: If I dump all this anger and resentment you say I have on my husband, he will be hurt. He will probably get angry back at me. He will be offended and pull farther away from me.

Me: He *will* be hurt, angry, and offended. I sure hope he is. Husbands only change when you scare them, rattle their cage, rock their world, and get their attention. He's like all the intimacy avoiders I have seen. He wants your marriage to stay the way it is and will only change if he must. When he feels your genuine hurt and anger and knows you will not continue to accept the way things are, *then* he will change. If you keep stuffing your emotions, he will never change because he won't see any need to change. If you vent your resentments, he will see how serious things are and be motivated to change. He will finally *get it.*

I urged her to write a letter to her husband—a letter with all her resentments expressed in living color. No holding back. *The truth—in love.* I asked her to write as much as she needed: "If it is forty pages long, so be it." I concluded by telling her I would have her read it at our next joint marital session.

I could tell by the look on her face that she wasn't going to do it. She said her pastor and a well-known Christian author she had been reading had recommended a different approach: forget the past, pray, quickly forgive her husband, and then focus on loving him unconditionally. Eventually he would come around and be the husband she had always dreamed he'd be. She thanked me for my time and said she wouldn't need any more of my services.

I fought the urge to gag. I wanted to say, "My dear lady, this approach you're going to try is the same approach you have been trying for years. How is it going so far?" Instead, trying to be the gracious psychologist, I wished her well and said to call me if she changed her mind.

I Hate It When I'm Right

Ten months later this same couple was sitting in front of me. But, oh, what a difference! This time the husband had called to make the appointment. He sat on the edge of my couch, nervous and sweating. The wife looked like a totally different woman. She was as cold as an Arctic blast. Her face was expressionless. She showed no emotion, except for irritation she was in my office. "She's hit the wall," I thought.

When she opened her mouth, she said exactly what I expected. She wanted out of their marriage. She had finally gotten sick and tired of living with this man. She had no feelings for him and didn't care about him. Period. She had only come today to try and get it through his thick skull that it was over. She had gotten an apartment, her own checking account, and an attorney. He would be served with divorce papers shortly. All she wanted from him was a friendly divorce.

Her husband was devastated. A shell of his former confident self. He finally "got it," but now it was too late. He finally sighed through tears, "Doc, you were right. I wish I would have listened." She never came back to therapy after that session. I saw him in about ten individual sessions, and we accomplished some good work together. Although he changed as a man and a husband, his wife couldn't have cared less. Her resentments were still bottled up inside, and they drove her away from him. Never wavering, she divorced him.

Chapter 9

Speak the Truth in Love

D o you think the story of the couple I described in chapter 8 is unusual? Do you think they are a rare exception? Do you think that losing your love for your husband and wanting out of your marriage could never happen? Think again. The resentments against your husband that you are holding inside are pushing you closer and closer to "the wall." Sooner or later you will smash into it. When you do, you won't care about him anymore.

You might stay married, and I hope you do. But you won't love him. At best you will tolerate him and go through the motions of being his wife. You will do it for the kids and out of obedience to God, but your heart won't be in it.

The Wife Who Wants Out

In the past ten years of my clinical practice I have seen a huge increase in the number of Christian wives who leave their husbands. The story is always the same. The wife works hard to be the best partner possible, hoping and praying that her IA will respond to her loving behavior by meeting her needs. Month after month, year after year, he doesn't. He doesn't listen, talk, romance her, and lead her spiritually. He just doesn't.

She gets hurt, frustrated, and angry each time he fails to love her the way she needs to be loved. Yet, being the good Christian wife, she chokes down these painful feelings and soldiers on.

Maybe tomorrow he will change, or next week. *Maybe* by Easter or Christmas. *Maybe* this coming Valentine's Day. *Maybe* after the pastor's series on marriage. *Maybe* after the marriage seminar. *Maybe* after he sees two of our close friends divorce. Maybe. Maybe. Maybe.

Each *maybe* that slips past with no change adds a little more rejection, disappointment, and hurt, adding a touch more anger to the growing pool of resentment in her heart. One day this "good Christian wife" wakes up and decides she's had enough! She is through with the *maybes* and through with him. She may have gone five, seven, or even twenty years, but she isn't going any further.

Her exit from the marriage seems terribly sudden, but it isn't. It has been coming slowly but surely for a long time. Her resentments have finally filled her heart, leaving no room for any love for that man who has—one hurt at a time—robbed her of her deepest desires in life.

You May Not Divorce, but You Will Suffer

Your stuffed resentments may not push you into divorce court. I fervently hope they don't. Still, they will cause you to suffer in many areas of your life.

Emotional pain

Your resentments will attack your psychological system. You may have heard that repressed anger leads to depression. That is true. It will provoke a broad range of emotional problems: depression; generalized anxiety; panic attacks; worry; insomnia; addictions to food, spending, and alcohol; lowered self-esteem; increased insecurities; or a pattern of negative thinking and cynicism.

Physical pain

Your pool of stuffed, negative feelings will travel to the weak areas of your body, wreaking havoc. Does your family have a history of heart trouble? That is where your resentments will go. I have observed resentments cause (or worsen) many physical diseases: kidney problems, back pain, migraines, chronic fatigue syndrome, irritable bowel syndrome, skin conditions, and arthritis.

Spiritual pain

As long as you continue to hold internal grudges against your husband, your relationship with God will suffer. God commands us to forgive others as He has forgiven us (Eph. 4:32; Col. 3:13), but you haven't forgiven your husband. If you don't forgive your husband, God won't forgive you (Matt. 6:14–15, 18:21–35; Mark 11:25–26). You desperately need to be close to your heavenly Father; your relationship with Him is precious and vital. Unexpressed grudges will separate you from God. You will still know Him and be His child, but you won't be close to Him.

Parental pain

Your resentments will seriously hamper your ability to love, nurture, and train your children. It takes a great deal of emotional and physical energy to interact with children every day. You won't have any reserves because you are spending all your energy keeping your grudges alive. You won't have patience as a mother and will often get irritable and angry with your kids. You will overreact, yell too much, and punish them too harshly.

Marital pain

Your pool of resentments will cause two major consequences in marriage. First, you won't be a good wife. Carrying around all your grudges against your husband will prevent you from fulfilling your God-given role as a wife. You won't be able to respect him, support him, submit to his leadership, be patient with him, or love him. Every time he makes a mistake, even a small one, it will energize your pool of grudges, and you will pull a little farther away.

The second consequence is that he won't change. If you never tell him exactly what he has done to hurt and offend you, he will never know. Since he has no idea what he has done, he will have no idea what he needs to change. I can't overemphasize this point: he will never *get it* without you telling him. Thinking your marriage is as good as it can be, he will remain an IA. You might as well get his headstone carved now:

> Here lies Clive
>
> He communicates as much now as when he was alive
>
> Born an intimacy avoider
>
> Lived an intimacy avoider
>
> Died an intimacy avoider

Can You Relate?

Does any of this sound familiar? Can you relate to the pain in these five areas? I'll bet you can. Like thousands of wives I have counseled in my office, at seminars, or via e-mail and phone, I will bet you have been living with pain for some time—way too long. It is time to stop the pain, get healthy, forgive, and give your IA husband a crystal-clear picture of what he is doing to cause you pain.

I know you are probably reluctant to open up and let all this pain out. You have some reservations, don't you? You want to make sure this is the right thing to do. I understand. Before I describe how to get rid of the pain, let me address what I see as your major concerns.

"But I don't hold any grudges!"

Please. Don't even go there. Men don't tend to hold grudges. We are not that sensitive and our memories are terrible. We forget everything. Women, however, hold grudges. You are sensitive creatures and can't help taking things personally. It is how God made you. You never forget anything. You remember every detail of past events, especially whenever they involved some kind of emotional pain.

You are still holding a grudge against Susie Finklemeyer, that ditzy redhead in fifth grade who told Bobby Bushwacker that you liked him. Aren't you? You can still remember and feel intensely the embarrassment when you realized Susie had finked on you. You were wearing your yellow, leopard-spotted sweater and standing in line at the lunch counter.

Be honest with yourself. One of the deepest longings of your heart is to be close to your husband. Each time he prevents that closeness from developing, it is a blow, an injury. It hurts and makes you angry. Don't deny it. Don't kid yourself into believing it is not that big a deal. It is a big deal. It is a huge, massive deal! That dream was strongest on the most important day of your life with all its memories: your wedding day.

Get out of denial. It is OK to admit that you are hurt and angry—even resentful—at your husband.

"But I've told him what upsets me!"

You may think you have already told him about your feelings regarding his lack of communication, romance, and leadership. Maybe you have, but I can say with absolute certainty he hasn't gotten the message. Your husband's brain is thick as a brick. The occasional comment about what he's doing wrong as a husband will glance off his Teflon, clueless skull. He forgot what you said thirty seconds later and went looking for the potato chip bag.

There is only one way to punch through his witlessness and get him to see right through to your heart pain. That is to give it to him straight, tough, direct, and *all at one time*. The whole emotional enchilada, right in the kisser. In a bit I will show you how to do that.

"What does the Bible say?"

I am glad you asked. My direct, confront-your-husband-with-the-truth approach is clearly taught in the Bible. That is where I got it. This isn't my idea; it is God's idea. Ephesians 4:26–27 commands us to:

> Be angry, and yet do not sin; do not let the sun go down on your anger, and do not give the devil an opportunity.

Paul is acknowledging that we all get angry, but we need to express that anger in the right way so we don't sin. If we hold anger in, we give the devil an open door to attack us. I believe Satan uses the resentment and bitterness created by our stuffed feelings to destroy us and our relationships. The only way to prevent this is to get the anger out. The sooner the better.

We are taught to "speak the truth in love" (Eph. 4:15, NLT). You have some important truths to tell your husband about what he has done to hurt you. In Galatians it says we should "bear one another's burdens" (Gal. 6:2). How can your husband bear your burdens if he has no idea what they are? You have to tell him!

The Bible instructs to confront another whenever something has happened that is negatively impacting a relationship (Matt. 5:23–24; 18:15–17). It may be something the other person has against us or something we have against the other person. It may be sin in the other person's life. Whatever the issue, we are to go and speak to that person directly.

The Bible provides example after example of confrontation:

- Samuel confronted King Saul (1 Sam. 15:1–35).

- Nathan confronted King David (2 Sam. 12:1–14).

- Jesus confronted the Pharisees (Matt. 23:13–36) and His disciples (Matt. 16:23; Mark 9:33–37).

- Jesus confronted Martha (Luke 10:38–42).

- Paul confronted Peter (Gal. 2:11).

Why is confronting your husband with the truth of your resentments so important? Because it cleans your system of negative, destructive emotions; leads to forgiveness; and promotes emotional, physical, and spiritual health. In addition, it will make you a better mother and help you continue loving your spouse and fulfilling God's role for you as his wife. Finally, it gets his attention and creates the possibility of change in your marriage.

That is *why* you do it. Here is *how* you do it.

Your Letter of Resentments

I want you to write your husband a letter expressing all the resentments you are holding against him. Go all the way back to the beginning—the day you met him. Think back over your history and pray that God will bring up all the painful memories that need to be flushed out. To purge the pain and genuinely heal and forgive, you must put down on paper what happened *and* describe how you feel about that.

Go into as much detail as possible about what he has done to anger, offend, hurt, and disappoint you. You will write out the events *and* the emotions they stirred. Details are important because your pain is connected to them. If you don't get the details out, you won't get your pain out. Plus you are dealing with a man. For him to get it and actually realize what it has been like to be his wife, you have to paint him a very clear picture.

You need to be nothing less than completely and brutally honest in this letter of resentments. You are going to give it to him straight, and you will not spare his feelings in any way. You will not let him down easy. You will not rationalize or excuse

117

his behavior. You will not blame the hurtful things he has done on his childhood, his personality, or his stressful job. You will not bring up *your* mistakes in the marriage. That will be done in another stage of the Husband Transformation process. All you will admit to now is enabling his mistakes by tolerating them.

This letter is going to be negative. Absolutely all of it. Do not—I repeat, do not—put any positives of any kind in the letter. Many "experts" recommend that in a confrontation you should compliment the other person because this softens the blow and helps him receive and act on your message. Here, they are wrong! Not even close to being right.

We don't want to soften the blow! If you patty-cake around by praising him, your message will be diluted. He will just hear the praise and think, "I'm not such a bad guy. She is not that upset. My mistakes aren't that serious." He won't get it. You will have wasted your time. You will be positive at other times in this strategy. *Not now.*

After hearing my explanation of this letter, wives often respond, "Oh, but I don't want to be too hard on him. I don't want him to be angry and upset." I tell them, "There is no way you can be too hard on him. Yes, you do want him to be angry and upset. Rattled. Shaken to the core. Blown away. I know husbands. If you give him only one positive comment, he will seize on that and remember nothing else you say."

You want this to be a letter he will never forget. A letter that will finally break through his "things are OK" wall and help him understand and feel your pain. A letter that will play a major role in changing his life.

You won't write this letter in one sitting. Digging deep and reliving the pain will be physically and emotionally exhausting. Chip away at it. Write for thirty minutes today, an hour tomorrow, forty-five minutes two days later, and so on. It may take a week or two to complete this message. Let it flow. Don't worry about grammar, punctuation, or spelling. This is from-the-gut, from-the-heart, let-it-all-hang-out writing.

The prelude

Go to your husband, sit him down, look him straight in his eyes, and say, "_____ (his name), I want to set up a meeting three days from now." (He will probably look sickened and think, "Oh no, not another meeting!") Then continue, "I'm ready for the next step in Dr. Clarke's strategy. I am going to tell you some very personal, difficult, and painful things. I don't want the kids in the house when I do it. Please arrange for someone else to watch them during this time."

Once you have scheduled the meeting, get up and leave. Do not tell him what you are planning; make him wait to find out. With this letter I prefer a surprise attack. If he already knows about the letter of resentments because he has read the book (this will be true of 0.4 percent of husbands), that is fine. He still won't know what you are going to say. Act just as you did before the meeting where you talked about your needs (chapter 4): cool, reserved, quiet, and to yourself.

The sting

For this meeting sit at your kitchen or dining room table, not a casual, comfortable place. You want a somber, serious tone. Next inform him of the ground rules: "As you can see, I have a letter I'm going to read. It is very important that you remain silent throughout. Please listen and do not interrupt. I want you to hear me and work hard to understand what I am saying and feeling. Walk in my shoes and see things from my point of view. This is *my* truth and *my* feelings. I will not argue over the details. I ask you to accept and validate my feelings and believe me. I have lived all of this, and it is an accurate description of my life with you." (You can deliver this message verbally or read it as the first paragraph of your letter).

If he refuses to listen or interrupts you more than once, hand him the letter and walk away. Most intimacy avoiders are decent sorts and will listen in silence.

Here is a sample letter of resentments. It contains the basic format that I recommend you use in creating your own unique document.

_____ (no "Dear," just his name).

It wasn't easy writing this letter, and it won't be easy for you to hear it. But it has to be done. Over the course of our relationship you have done a number of things that have hurt me deeply. I don't think you have any idea how much pain you have caused. In fact, you're still doing things that hurt me.

I realized recently that I am still holding on to these painful memories and the emotions that go with them. I stuffed them down, and they are inside me. I still resent you for all the mistakes you have made. That is not good for me, and it is not good for our relationship. So it is time for me to get these resentments out.

As I read this letter, just listen. Don't say anything. I want to heal from the damage you have done to me. I want to forgive you. I want you to know what you have done and to feel some of the pain I have felt. I want you to change and stop hurting me. I'm going to begin at the beginning of our relationship.

Remember Darlene, your old girlfriend? I do. I haven't been able to forgive you for contacting her after you and I had been going out for three months. I was falling in love with you. We were a couple, and I thought you cared for me.

I will never forget that moment when I heard Darlene's voice on your answering machine, talking about your date the night before. You told me you were through with her! I have carried the betrayal, anger, and deep hurt over Darlene up to this day. How could you do that? Why didn't you just tell me that you wanted to date Darlene? That would have hurt too, but it would have been less painful than you doing it behind my back. I felt like a fool. I had placed my heart in your hands, and you crushed it. I don't think I have ever completely trusted you since then. I'm telling you now so I can release the pain and truly forgive you.

About six months before we got married, we started having sex. I freely admit my responsibility in this sin. You didn't force me. I wanted to do it. But it was wrong. I'm ashamed of myself for giving to you something God wanted me to give only after marriage. We violated a boundary set down by God, and we have paid for it. I'm convinced that our struggles in the areas of trust and sex stem, in part, from premarital sex. I am angry with you for not protecting me sexually. It was your job as the man to make sure we didn't go too far. I accept my responsibility for it, so I want you to accept yours. I know I didn't think so at the time, but I have come to realize that you violated me. It hurts me deeply that you didn't respect me enough to save intercourse until after our wedding.

Over the years your workaholism has caused me a great deal of grief, anguish, and anger. Your job has always been your number-one priority. Do you know what it is like to wait, day after day and month after month and year after year, for your husband to come home? Do you know what it is like to know you are not as important to your husband as his stupid job?

I won't mention every time you were late for dinner, social plans, special events at the kids' schools, and birthday parties. I don't have enough pen and paper. But I will mention two that stand out.

Susie's sixth birthday party. It was the first time that we had both sets of grandparents in town for a birthday. You promised you would be home by five o'clock. You lied, just like you lied a thousand other times about when you'd come home. I was angry and humiliated that night as we waited an hour and a half for you to show up. Not even a phone call. Couldn't you have told your client that you had to be at your daughter's birthday party? You hurt your daughter and me that day.

The second is our thirteenth wedding anniversary. We had made some very special plans for that night: the theater and then dinner. I was so looking forward to seeing that play with you. But once again your job was more important. You called to say you were hung up with a client problem and we would have to miss the play. I was furious and, at the same time, brokenhearted. Another promise shattered.

I have tolerated your workaholism for years. I have "understood." I have covered for you with our friends and the kids, and bitten my tongue a million times when you have chosen your job over me. No more. I have forgiven you for all you've done up to now in this area.

From now on I am not going to resent you for working too much. That is because I am going to tell you what I think and feel every time you put your job first. I am going to tell the kids the truth when you're late: "Dad is a workaholic, and he loves his job more than he loves us." I won't save your dinner anymore. If you are late for a date or a social engagement, I will leave without you. I won't resent you another day for your workaholism. I will express my feelings and take action.

Five years ago you had lunch with Samantha, your sales assistant. When you told me, I couldn't believe you had done it. I also couldn't believe you thought it was no big deal. You and I had a deal: no lunches or dinners with a member of the opposite sex. If it's a group, that is OK but not one on one. I know you work with women. Guess what? I work with men. But if you have business with a woman, do it over the phone or in an office.

I believe nothing happened between you and Samantha. But something happened to my trust that day. What you did was wrong, and it hurt me. It reminded me of Darlene and how you had cheated on me with her. I forgive you for

Samantha, but I want you to never do this kind of thing again.

Your lack of romance over the years has really, really hurt me. You know from my letter of needs how important this is to me. I will never feel loved by you unless you romance me regularly. You romanced me during our courtship, then dropped it about three months into the marriage.

You don't send me flowers. You don't give me cards. You don't tell me I'm beautiful. You don't give me affection. You don't take me out once a week for a romantic date. You don't plan getaway weekends. You don't watch romantic movies with me. Your lack of romance makes me feel unloved and unattractive. I have wondered for years if you don't romance me because you're not attracted to me anymore. Do you still love me? Without romance I don't know.

When we do have a romantic time, I plan it. You know something? I am tired of doing that. It spoils it if I am always the one who makes it happen. I am frustrated and just plain angry with you for being such a nonromantic stick. Pursue me! Romance me! Love me!

Last year I planned that romantic, candlelight dinner for us. One more time I had hoped to spark some passion between us. I shouldn't have been surprised you were late getting home, but I was. I was also very angry and profoundly sad. You were distracted during dinner and didn't have much to say. Before I could mention my plan to go into the bedroom for a time of sexual intimacy, you went into the den and started watching a football game. I cried myself to sleep that night. Did you even notice? No.

Three years ago on Valentine's Day—for once—I decided to make no plans. I wanted to know if you would notice and come up with your own idea for this special night. You did nothing—nothing at all. You knew it was Valentine's Day, and yet you did nothing. I was exasperated and wounded. You told me you figured I didn't want to do anything because I hadn't mentioned it. Do I even have to mention that Valentine's Day is important to me?

I want and need romance, and not just on Valentine's Day and our anniversary. All the time. It is your job, and I want you to do it. Every time you blow it, I will vent my feelings with you. I will not suffer in silence anymore.

As for communication I could write forty pages on this topic alone. You don't talk to me about personal things. All I get is stuff about work, kids, friends, church activities, or home repairs. I am starving for closeness with you! That is why I married you! I need to know what you're thinking and feeling inside. Not knowing just kills me. It just kills me!

I can't count the number of times I have tried to get you to open up and share with me on a deeper level, only to have you shut down. I can't adequately express in words how frustrated, helpless, and disgusted this makes me feel.

Remember that weekend we had last summer at the beach? Of course, *I* set it up. No kids. Just the two of us. I wanted to talk with you. Really talk. Catch up, connect on a deeper level. You wanted sex. I gave you sex in the hope that in return you would open up and talk. You didn't. I resent you for that time and all the other times you have clammed up and refused to let me inside your head and heart.

I know that it is hard for you to communicate. I don't care. I know you weren't raised to open up and share yourself. I don't care. I know most husbands don't do it. I don't care. I need you to do it. As you guys like to shout at your all-male rallies: "Man up!"

I need to say something else about sex. For years I have resented you for only being warm and loving during inter-course. That is not enough for me! It makes sex into a chore—something else I do for you. I need emotional connection and romance in order to be a good partner and enjoy it myself. I'm telling you here and now that our sex life will be affected if you don't learn to communicate with me and meet my emotional needs.

There is another reason I haven't been interested in sex for years: your critical comments about my weight. I know I'm a little overweight. I don't need you to tell me. Your comments cut me like a knife. I have felt devastated and guilty because of my extra pounds. You make me feel like a fat lady who isn't good enough for you. Don't you know that a woman's body changes after giving birth to two kids? The only comment I ever want to hear from you about my appearance is, "You're beautiful." If you can't say that, then just say nothing at all.

It is one of my deepest disappointments that you have not been my spiritual partner and leader. I so want to share Christ with you, but you have shown no interest in this part of our marriage. Going to church with me is good, but it isn't good enough. I need to know how your walk with the Lord is going. What is He teaching you? What are your spiritual victories and defeats? What are you learning in your quiet times and Bible reading?

I have asked you these questions and you either give vague answers or ignore me. I have asked to pray with you, but you find ways to avoid that. I am bitter, resentful, and sad that we are not spiritually intimate. I am more than willing to be an equal partner in the spiritual area. All you need to do is initiate regular spiritual meetings and be willing to learn how to spiritually bond with me.

Well, that is it for all my resentments. With God's help I am going to forgive you for all these things I have expressed. Now I will close with four important wrap-up points.

First, you don't have to respond to this letter now. It is a lot to take in. In fact, I don't want you to respond right away. I will hand it over to you when I'm done reading and you can reread it by yourself. When you are ready to talk about what I have shared, please let me know, and we'll set up a meeting. I want you to know that I want your heartfelt apology for all these hurtful behaviors. I want you to explain, the best way you can, why you have treated me this way. I want you to convince me that you understand what I have been through and that you are willing to work to make changes. I anticipate having a number of conversations about this letter, but I won't ask you to talk. You need to come to me.

Second, if you have resentments against me, I want you to express them. You need to first deal with my resentments and help me feel understood. Then please write a letter to me sharing your resentments. Please do not write a letter refuting the points I made in mine. If you have bona fide beefs against me, put those down on paper.

Third, there will be times when I will come to you and express more painful feelings about the areas I brought up in my letter. Writing this letter has helped me take a huge step toward forgiveness, but I will still need to do some follow-up venting here and there. Please just listen and help me feel understood.

Fourth, as I have indicated several times, from now on I will be much more honest and expressive with you when you do something to anger and hurt me. As soon as possible after the painful event, I will tell you my feelings. You don't have to respond. Just listen and understand. I will express myself this way to keep my system clean, to avoid building up more resentments, to keep on forgiving you, and to continue to make my needs clear to you.

_____ (no "Love," just your name)

Pretty brutal, huh? Long, detailed, and gut-level honest. And brutal. Your intimacy avoider will begin to crack and splinter after you read him your letter. I have seen this kind of letter lead to healing and forgiveness in wives and to husbands who are motivated to change. That may seem like the impossible dream, but it isn't. So sit down today and start writing. You will be glad you did.

Chapter 10

Yeah, I'm Talking to You

OK, YOU HAVE just finished reading your letter of resentments, and you can tell by the expression on your husband's face that you've gotten his attention. He doesn't look like a deer in the headlights. No, he is way past that. He looks like a deer that's been hit by the car behind the headlights. He has entered... The Twilight Zone. He's wondering whatever happened to his sweet, kind, she's-practically-a-saint-and-never-rocked-the-boat-before wife. This is bad. Really bad.

You've made a good start, but it's only a start. You want to make sure this is much more than just a moment in time or a flash flood that temporarily pushes him off the road to intimacy avoidance and into a ditch. Remember, IAs are masters of the rapid recovery. Don't let him recover and begin to feel comfortable. Don't let him make promises and then, after two weeks, revert to the same old routine.

You have to maintain your edge. You have to keep him *on edge*. You must force him off the dead-end road he is on and onto another, better road—the road to becoming a loving, more expressive husband. In the meantime you must keep on being the "new you." The "I'm going to tell you the way it is every time" you. A better, healthier you. Keep going. It just might lead to a better husband.

One-Way Communication

How do you get him off the wrong road and onto the right one? By continuing to be upfront, honest, and straightforward using one-way communication. One-way communication is going directly to your IA and *briefly* telling him the truth about your thoughts and emotions concerning something that has happened in your relationship. I call it one-way because *you* do all the talking.

You tell him he doesn't have to respond. Just ask him to listen and understand, take time to process what you've said, and find you and share his reaction when he's ready. When you are done talking, simply go silent. If you are at home, walk away. If you are in the car, a restaurant, or out somewhere, be quiet for at least five minutes. After that you can continue in silence or bring up another topic of conversation. You speak your piece, and you move on.

Unlike what you've done in the past, you do not press him for an immediate reaction. Why not? Two reasons:

1. Men cannot respond right away. They need time to process and figure out their feelings and thoughts on an issue. A personal issue takes them even longer.

2. When they feel pressured by a woman, men will always clam up and say nothing. They feel controlled and show you with their silence that you can't make them talk.

If you express yourself in *two minutes or less* and allow him time to process, there is a chance your IA will consider what you say and get back to you to continue the conversation. If you badger him or even ask him nicely for an immediate response, your IA will harden up and never respond. Never. My one-way communication strategy prompts a "maybe." Your natural-wife way of pushing him to say something back right away gets you a "never." Try my way.

Do the Two-Step When He Doesn't Return

What if you try one-way communication and he still doesn't come back with a response? Since he is an IA, that is likely to happen often. When you have waited a day or two and it is pretty clear he has no intention of reacting, take two steps.

Step one: Give him one low-key, unemotional reminder. You get only one. If you remind him twice, you turn into a nagging witch. Try this: "Remember that issue we discussed? When you are ready, I would like you to find me and give me your reaction to what I said." After these two statements, say nothing else about it. Move on.

Step two: If he still won't talk about it, go to him and give him a one-way communication that expresses your feelings about his decision to ignore you and refusal to respond. It'll go something like this: "I'm angry and disappointed that you have chosen to not come back to me about (whatever issue you had brought up). It makes me feel unloved and unimportant. I just wanted you to know." Then drop it. Walk away. Don't bring it up again.

The Seven Keeps of One-Way Communication

There are many benefits of one-way—do it when you need to do it—communication. I call these the Seven Keeps:

1. It *keeps* your system clean of negative, destructive emotions such as anger, hurt, bitterness, and resentment. You get the pain your husband causes out of you, and you stay healthy—emotionally, physically, and spiritually.

2. It ensures that you *keep* on forgiving your husband for his mistakes. The letter of resentments is

a crucial step, but you have to continue to flush out daily pain. If you don't, it will turn into resentment, and you will develop another nasty pool of negative, debilitating emotions.

3. It *keeps* your needs and the behaviors that bother you in full view of your husband. Every time you vent one-way, he is reminded of the things you consider most important in the marriage.

4. It *keeps* him off balance and uncomfortable, which is the only time he will change.

5. It provides you the opportunity to *keep* teaching your husband the skills he needs to love you: how to correct his weaknesses, how to understand why he is the way he is, how to stop hurting you, how to open up and communicate what is inside.

6. It *keeps* alive the possibility that he will listen to you, "get" what you're saying, think about it, and respond—at least some of the time. When you drop your verbal payload (not being furious, just honest) and leave, he may eventually follow you. He doesn't like it when you're upset with him, so he's likely to come after you.

7. Most importantly, one-way communication *keeps* you following Scripture.

The verses I use to support the letter of resentments are the same verses that support one-way communication. The Bible teaches us to "be angry, and yet do not sin" (Eph. 4:26), "speak the truth in love" (Eph. 4:15, NLT), "bear one another's burdens" (Gal. 6:2), and confront others (Matt. 5:23–24; 18:15–17).

You need to learn how to do one-way communication in five categories. What follows is a crash course. I will review them one at a time, briefly describing the category and listing several examples.

Bring Up Past Pain

The deep hurts your husband has caused you cannot be expressed and forgiven quickly. While the letter of resentments is a significant step toward healing, it will not be enough. Your heart will heal over time as you periodically share with your husband leftover pain connected to these events. Pray that God will bring up the pain so you can flush it out. It can be triggered any number of ways: a careless comment, a behavior that reminds you of how he hurt you years before, a song on the radio, a movie, or God just bringing the traumatic event to mind. When the pain comes up, go to your husband and vent it, using one-way communication such as this:

Example 1. Wife: I need to talk about Darlene again.

"Just listen and help me feel understood. I don't want you to say anything original now. Be with me and hear me. When I saw a woman this morning who looked like Darlene, the pain of what you did came flooding back. I still have a hard time believing you went back to her. That hurts way down deep. When we're not getting along, I automatically doubt your commitment. I wonder if you would prefer being with Darlene or some other woman. I thought today that what would help me get over her is to feel closer to you. If we could talk—I mean really talk—I think I could believe you love me and want only me. Thanks for listening. If you want to get back to me with a response, let me know. It's up to you."

Example 2. Wife: I have something I need to say to you.

"This last month you have slipped back into workaholic mode. No, don't give me any excuses! Just hear me out. I know it is a busy time at work. Guess what? It is a busy time at home too.

I feel angry and frustrated, like I'm very unimportant to you. I need you here helping me, loving me, talking with me, and being my partner. When you work too much, it reminds me of all the times you have put work ahead of me and our family. This past month has brought up a lot of that old pain for me. I am tired of being number six on your priority list. I am angry, sad, and hurt that you can't seem to put me where I belong, which is at the top of your relationship list. Think about it. Get back to me if you want."

Stay Current

Chances are good that your husband will continue to make mistakes and cause you pain. That is life with a man—especially an intimacy avoider. To stay healthy, build respect, and keep your needs in front of his face, you must daily go to him and clean out your pain. He won't like it. That's tough, but it is good for both of you and for your relationship. Because it is one-way, he will be much better able to take in what you say and act on it.

Example 1. Wife: Do you have a minute?

"I wanted you to know that your comment this morning about my housekeeping made me angry and offended me. I do my best and your criticism really stung. I need praise and help with the chores, not sarcastic barbs. When you are ready, I would appreciate an apology."

Example 2. Wife: I needed you last night and you weren't there for me.

"I had had a stressful day. I wanted to vent to you and be comforted. But you half-listened for five minutes then turned on the television. I am angry and disappointed in you. I need you to listen to me every day."

Example 3. Wife: Just give me one minute to say something.

"Don't respond right now, just listen. Another week has gone by and you didn't schedule any time for us to talk. I am angry with you because even though you know this is an important need for me, you did nothing. I do not want to build up resentment against you, so I'm sharing my feelings."

Example 4. Wife: It has been two weeks since you promised to schedule a meeting for us with a financial adviser.

"You have chosen not to do it. Hold your excuses. I don't want to hear them. I feel angry, hurt, and betrayed. If you have no intention of seeing an adviser, say so. At least that would be honest."

Example 5. Wife: I have to tell you how I feel about the sex we had last night.

"Although I agreed, I regret giving in to you. In the week leading up to yesterday, you didn't romance me. I had no emotional connection to you because we hadn't talked on a deeper level. I need to feel loved and close to you in order to fully participate in sex. I feel used and cheap. I am angry because you got what you wanted, but I didn't get what I needed. Our sex is boring and a chore for me. It hurts me and pushes me away from you. If you want me to enjoy intercourse and be an active sexual partner, you have to meet my emotional and spiritual needs first."

Respond to His Classic IA Shtick

In the past your responses to his intimacy avoider behaviors have proved ineffective. When he killed conversation after conversation with his standard avoidance, you cried. Yelled. Lectured. Whispered. Begged. Pleaded. Reasoned. Threatened. Ignored. Nothing has worked. He is still an IA, and you are still a wife lacking intimacy.

It is time to try something new—something with a much

better chance of working. I want you to respond to his classic "IA shtick" with brief, verbal surgical strikes. The choreographed one-way responses below will rattle your man and create real change in your relationship. Plus these snappy comebacks will keep you sane and give you some fun. After all, when you live with an IA, you need some entertainment!

IA: He's not listening to you. His eyes are glazed over. He's "in the zone."

"Brain cramp, huh? I am insulted and angry because you're not paying attention to me. If you don't want to listen to me, say so. Let me know when you are ready to listen." (Stop talking and make him come to you to restart the conversation.)

IA: He falls silent as you talk. He gives no responses at all.

"You're not saying anything. I can't tell if you are listening. If you don't want to talk about this, tell me. If you are OK with this topic, give me some responses so I will know you're with me. It is frustrating to talk and get no feedback, so I won't do it. I will wait for you to tell me what is on your mind."

IA: He's not completely shut down, but his mind is somewhere else. The clue: his one- and two-word answers.

"You seem out of it tonight. You are not involved in this conversation. I won't keep trying to get you interested in what I'm saying. I will just get angry and so will you. Come to me when you are ready to talk. I would like to know what you're thinking about tonight, but you'll have to decide to tell me."

IA: He has dropped one of his logical conversation-killer comments on you: "You shouldn't feel that way." "You're too intense." "You're overreacting." "Simmer down, and I'll show you the facts." "You're wrong, and I can prove it." "Here's how to fix your problem." And on and on.

"Hold it right there. I don't need logic and I'm not going to listen to any right now. If I did, I would get furious. What I need is for you to listen to me, reflect what I'm saying, and help me feel understood. When you are ready to do that, let me know. Once I feel understood, then I'll be happy to listen to your logic."

IA: You asked, "How was your day?" and he replied, "Fine," or "OK."

"That one word really doesn't tell me too much. I need more information than that. Take some time and think about your day, then find me and tell me what you come up with."

IA: It is obvious that he is upset about something because in response to your reasonable question: "What's wrong?" he says, "Nothing."

"Please don't insult me. I know something is wrong. I know it is hard for you to talk about it, so I won't try to pry it out of you. I want to comfort and support you, but I can't if you don't tell me what's bothering you. When you want to share what it is, come tell me."

IA: "I don't know."

"When you do, come and find me and tell me. We can't build a conversation on 'I don't knows.'"

IA: "I don't want to talk about it."

"OK. I respect that. Please listen to me talk about it for five minutes. Hear me out. You don't have to give me your view now. After you think about what I've said and you're ready to talk, find me."

IA: "This isn't a good time to talk about it."

"What if I told you 'This isn't a good time' the next time you want sex? What sex is to you, communication is to me. When you are ready to talk about this issue, find me."

Connect the Dots

Just as your IA needs to be called on the carpet when he hurts you, he needs to be *praised* when he steps out of his IA role and does something positive. Men literally thrive on praise, especially from their wives. This is an effective way to shape a husband's behavior. However, don't just praise his behavior and drop it. After praising what he does, tell him specifically how his positive behavior has produced a loving response from you.

Your husband won't see the connection between his loving behavior and your response. He needs to appreciate the value of that connection because it will motivate him to keep on behaving the way you need. Tell him in detail that because:

- He loved you in a specific way,
- Shared something personal,
- Acted in a romantic way,
- Prayed with you, or
- Met another one of your needs...you did something loving for him in return.

Connect the dots for him every single time: "When you did A for me, I did B for you."

Example 1

"I put in extra effort preparing this meal because you did those three nasty chores for me yesterday." (Don't kid yourself; one of the ways to a man's heart is through his stomach.)

Example 2

"Do you want to know why I asked you for sex and was more responsive just now in bed? It isn't just because you have the body of a Greek god. It is because you initiated that talk time last night and spent twenty minutes in conversation with me." (Message: more talk equals more and better sex.)

Example 3

"I'm rubbing your feet now because two hours ago you listened to my long story about the conflict with my girlfriend. I needed to vent, and you were there."

Example 4

"Do you know why I just sat through that action-adventure movie with you? It isn't because I like to see bombs going off, people screaming in terror, and dead bodies flying around. I did it for you because three days ago you sat with me and watched that Cary Grant chick flick on television."

Example 5

"When you prayed with me just now, I felt so loved by you. It makes me love and respect you more. When we pray together, I see you as my protector, my leader, and my hero. It makes me want to do all kinds of loving things for you." (Do several loving behaviors in the next few days and tell him it's because he prayed with you.)

I know what you are thinking right now: "Why do I have to praise him *every time*? Shouldn't he do these behaviors just because they're the right things to do and because God commands him to do them?" Yes, he should do these things for those reasons. But the fact is, your connect-the-dots praise will be a huge motivating factor in his dropping the IA routine and doing what you need him to do. Don't quibble and get hung up on technicalities. Go ahead and praise him in this strategic way, and it will be well worth your efforts. And as you will see in a forthcoming chapter, praising your husband is a biblical principle.

Tell Him Why He Does What He Does

Your IA has zero insight into why he acts the way he does with you. After all, in his mind he is a *pretty good husband.* Why fix what isn't broken? While it is good to convince him your relationship is broken, that is not good enough. Left to himself he still won't figure out why he sidesteps closeness and consistently fails to meet your most important needs. Seeking an explanation for his poor relationship skills would mean digging into personal matters—and he has spent his whole life staying away from that sensitive arena.

With well-placed, one-way observations, your goal is to show him the reasons why he is intimacy-challenged: he is relationship-disabled. Having a coach to show him exactly where it originates is an integral part of the rehabilitation process. You are that coach. Even though he is not asking for your help, give it to him anyway. Your communication in this one-way area will set the stage for some crucial work you will ask him to complete a few steps further into my Husband Transformation Strategy.

Example 1

"That temper outburst last night reminded me of your dad. You look and act just like him when you lose it. Until you deal with him and your feelings about how he raised you, you will keep on raging—and hurting me and the kids."

Example 2

"When I said no to sex this morning, you shut me out and ignored me for three hours. You still haven't healed from your ex-wife rejecting you, sexually and in other ways. So when you feel like I have rejected you, you close down and won't talk about it. When you're ready, I want you to talk to me about what she did

138

to you. When that pain is out of you, you'll be able to open up to me and receive all my love."

Example 3

"You're stuffing your work stress again tonight. You have the TV on and have avoided me for the last two hours. I am hurt and frustrated. If you would share your work problems with me, you would be happier, and we would be closer. But that's up to you."

Example 4

"For the past month you have pulled back from me. I can see that you are preoccupied with your work and sports. You don't seem too happy with me or your life. I think one of the reasons is that you have drifted from the Lord. You are not having regular quiet times and have missed church several Sundays. I'm hurt by you shutting me out. I'm also concerned about you. If you want to talk about what is going on and want my help to get back on track spiritually, find me and we'll talk."

Example 5

"Did you notice what you just did? Our conversation was starting to get a little personal, and you made a joke to lighten the mood. You do that a lot. It ticks me off because I need closeness with you. I have seen your dad and brother do the same thing to avoid personal subjects. I would like to talk about this and what we can do about it. When you are ready, let me know and we'll schedule a talk time."

You won't be good at this one-way communication approach for a while. No one is naturally gifted at this process. It usually takes two to three months to get the hang of it. Practice. Practice. Practice. Your husband will give you many opportunities to hone your one-way skills. Try rereading this chapter several times and discuss your progress with a few members of your support team. Most importantly pray for God's help.

Remember: be honest, be brief, and tell him not to respond

right away. Get in, say what you need to say, and get out. Even after your intimacy avoider makes significant changes, you must continue to use one-way communication with him for the rest of your marriage. It will prevent him from slipping back into IA mode and help maintain the intimacy you have worked so hard to create.

Now that you have let it all hang out with your husband, buckle your seat belt and get ready for a bumpier road. No wife can blame all of her marital problems on her spouse. It is time to face facts and take the next step. You must uncover what behavior of yours is killing any hope of intimacy with your husband. This won't feel as satisfying as venting your feelings, but steps four and five will take you down the challenging road of self-examination.

STEP FOUR

I NEED TO KNOW EXACTLY HOW I AM KILLING OUR INTIMACY

Chapter 11

What Do I Do
That Shuts You Up?

I HAVE BEEN SEEING couples in therapy for twenty-five years. Ninety-nine percent of all first sessions follow the same pattern. After taking a brief history of each person's background, I ask, "Tell me why you've come to see me."

Immediately one spouse launches into a recitation of the other spouse's faults. I listen for five minutes as this spouse rakes the other over the coals, covering every possible mistake he or she has made. Then I interrupt (and believe me, I have to interrupt) and say, "That's enough. I get the picture."

Turning to the other spouse, I say, "OK, your turn." That spouse typically starts weeping and responds, "All those charges are true! I'm guilty of every one of them! Guilty, I tell you! I'm a pathetic excuse for a husband/wife!" That spouse goes to his/her knees and begs for a chance to change.

Right. Like that is ever going to happen.

You know what really happens. The other launches into a litany of the first spouse's weaknesses and mistakes. After another five minutes I say again, "That's enough." Then I give my little speech that is the actual beginning of marital therapy, which goes like this: "You've done an excellent job describing each other's faults. You're both right. We will address all the issues you mentioned, but focusing solely on your partner won't lead to real change in your marriage. Change comes when you look in the mirror, admit your faults, and make the conscious decision to work on them. So let's hear what each of you has done wrong in this relationship."

Oh, they don't like that. They don't like that at all. But I know what I am doing. It is fair and very important that you tell your partner what you want him/her to change. Yet it is equally important to face your own contributions to marital problems and do your own changing.

Your Turn in the Hot Seat

Women, to this point in my Husband Transformation Strategy the central focus has been your husband—the needs in your life you want him to meet, the mistakes he has made that have hurt you and caused resentment, and the changes you would like *him* to make.

As I have indicated, zeroing in on your husband is the best way to begin. If you start by revealing all your weaknesses, he will quickly write the whole thing off as your problem. So prior to this you have gone after your husband in a very direct, upfront way. And you will keep being honest with him about your needs and what *he* can do to improve your relationship.

However, the time has come to shift the focus to you. It is *your turn* in the hot seat. While there is no question that your husband does things that kill intimacy, get ready for some bad news: so do you. Yes, you! Even though you are the partner in the relationship who is working as hard as possible to achieve intimacy, you are just as guilty of snuffing it out.

Without realizing it, you are enabling your intimacy avoider to remain an IA. You are doing specific behaviors that turn your husband off, push him away from you, and shut him up. I know you don't want to destroy opportunities for closeness with your husband, but that is what you're doing. What you must do is discover what behaviors of yours are killing your hopes of achieving intimacy and then eliminate them. Here is how to proceed.

Please, tell me the truth about me.

Go to your husband and tell him you want to schedule a meeting. He will likely cringe and say, "No! Not another meeting!" Give him your best smile and reply, "Don't worry, honey, I think you're going to like this one. It's not about your mistakes. It's about *my* mistakes." Don't give him any more information, and set a meeting three or four days later.

At this meeting there are five messages you want to deliver. Here they are, in the order in which they are to be communicated:

1. I've been honest with you.

"Honey, as you know, I've been brutally honest with you over the past several weeks. I've shared my needs. I've shared my resentments over your actions in the past that really hurt and angered me. I haven't held back anything. I haven't softened the blow."

2. I'll keep being honest with you.

"For the rest of our marriage I'm going to keep on being honest. When you do or say something that significantly bothers me, I'm going to tell you. That's good for me, and it lets you know what I need from you."

3. Be honest with me.

"Now I want you to be honest with me. I want you to tell me what *I* do to stop you from being the husband I need you to be. Although you're half of our marriage problems, I'm the other half. I know I've done things in the past to hurt you, offend you, and turn you away from me. I know I do things now, every week, that bug you and keep you from opening up and talking with me. I know I'm guilty of killing our chances for intimacy, but I don't know exactly what these things are. You do.

"Honey, I need you to tell me what these things are. When I know what I'm doing wrong, I'll be able to stop making these mistakes. Don't tell me now (as though he would, anyway). Take this next week and think and pray about it. Don't worry about hurting my feelings. Go for it. Don't spare me. Let me have it. I want to know. I need to know."

Do not tell him at this first meeting what mistakes you think you have made. It is important that he work on this assignment himself, without any help from you.

4. Here's what I want from you.

"There are three areas I want you to cover in your response. I'll tell you what they are. Then, so you have something to refer to, I'll give you this three-by-five card with the three points written on it. Please write down your answers so your message is clear and I can have a written record to refer to.

"First, tell me what I have done to you in the past to offend and hurt you. (If he has already written a letter of resentments, you can skip this category. Being an IA, he probably hasn't done this, so you will need to ask for his resentments again.) Go all the way back to the beginning of our relationship. I harbored grudges against you for years. I'll bet you have some grudges against me too. Please write them down.

"Second, let me know what I do these days to turn you off and shut you up. Be as specific as you can: my behavior, my words, my attitude, whatever. How do I irritate you and prevent you from talking personally with me and meeting my needs?

"Third, describe what I can do, specifically, to help you open up and be closer to me. I know there are actions I can take that you'd love me to do. Actions that would help you talk to me, pray with me, and be a team player with the kids and the housework."

5. If necessary I'll talk to others.

"Sweetheart, if you can't come up with specifics for me next week, I'll do my best to gather information on my mistakes from our kids, family members, and friends. These persons are close to us and have seen me interact with you many times." (Sometimes a husband will work harder on this assignment because he would rather you not talk to others about your marital issues.)

Schedule the next meeting for one week in the future. Close by asking him to pray with you about this step in the program. If he won't, go ahead and say a brief prayer—out loud—asking the Lord to help him write down the mistakes you have made and are still making that kill your intimacy.

How to Kill Intimacy

Before the next meeting spend some time taking a good hard look at yourself. Without talking to anyone, think about how you kill intimacy with your husband. What do you do that prevents him from connecting with you on a deeper level? After praying about this, brainstorm and write down all the possible ways you turn him away from conversation, romance, and treating you the way you want to be treated.

To help you with this task, I have included below four common ways wives kill intimacy. I describe each killer pattern and what you can do to change it. See if you recognize yourself in any of the following descriptions.

The sweetheart of the rodeo

You are "the good little woman" who accepts her husband just the way he is, even though he doesn't share personal feelings, you are not a priority in his life, and he is about as romantic as a block of wood and has no idea of your personal needs. Unhappy in marriage, you feel as if you are living with a nice, decent male roommate, and don't know him that well. Your marital relationship can be described as safe, stable, superficial, and...boring. So boring it has killed any hopes of ever forging deeper, more passionate bonds.

OK, cowgirl, if you believe your husband can't change and are tolerating a mediocre marriage, then you are part of the problem. You are enabling him to remain an intimacy avoider! Since he knows you are OK with who he is and will never demand he change, he has zero motivation to do anything differently.

If you have been the sweetheart of the rodeo, it is time to hang up your cowgirl hat and spurs! Stop being so nice, forgiving, and fake all the time. Let the other "sweethearts" you know continue to grin and bear their IAs. Choose instead to believe three truths: 1) you can wield tremendous power and influence in your IA's life, 2) he can change, and 3) you should never waver in your commitment to follow the strategy in this book.

The nagging witch

You are way too aggressive in your attempts to get your man to open up and talk personally. In your drive to get some intimacy with your man, you are too direct and apply too much pressure. You pepper him with questions, press him for responses, and insist he tell you what he thinks and feels—right now! You bring up the same topic repeatedly in the hope that he will finally give you an answer. If he won't respond, you follow him down the hall, yakking away and pressing for a response.

You are a nagging witch, and without realizing it, you are killing conversations and robbing yourself of the intimacy you so desperately desire. You constantly back your husband into conversational corners. He feels threatened and controlled. Not surprisingly he won't yield any dialogue. Instead he clams up and says nothing, snaps at you in anger and frustration, or leaves the room. Sound familiar?

Your style of trying to force your husband to communicate is a complete failure. It only succeeds in shutting him up and driving him farther away. He thinks you are attacking his manhood and independence. You know something? *He is right.* Your intensity becomes the only issue in his mind. As he fends off your high-pressure approaches, the thoughts rocketing through his brain are things such as:

- "What a nag!"

- "What is her problem?"

- "Back off!"

- "I just want to get away from this Screaming Meemie!"

You may be a nagging witch who periodically turns into a volcano. You stuff, stuff, stuff your frustration, anger, and hurt over your husband's lack of communication. Finally you get filled up to your eyebrows with pain and erupt. You blast him with a verbal barrage of rage, disappointment, and bitterness. Critical, sarcastic, and belittling, you want to hurt him the same way he hurts you. Believe me, you do hurt him. But in doing so, you push him even further away.

The cure for nagging witches is to practice the one-way communication technique I explained in the previous chapter. (You may have just read it, but it won't hurt to take a quick refresher course.) Stop pressing him for responses. Develop the healthy habit of going to him, expressing what you want to say—briefly, directly, and honestly—and walking away. Tell him your needs and walk away. Share your feelings when he hurts or angers you, and walk away. If you struggle to control your intensity with certain topics, write a note and give it to him, and then walk away.

She who can't be pleased

Like most wives, you assume your husband knows exactly what your needs are and chooses not to meet them. Without giving him any clues, you expect him to somehow figure out what you need and come through for you. You think, "If he really loved me, he would just know what I need." Not only are you living in a fantasy world, but you are also being unfair to your husband.

As I mentioned in chapter 4, your husband has no idea what your needs are. Here is a man who can't find his shoes in the morning. A man who is about as sensitive and intuitive as a marble paperweight. A man who doesn't even know what *his* real needs are. How in the world do you expect him to identify and meet your needs?

My wife, Sandy, has been just as guilty as you in this area of expecting too much of a husband. Here is one small example. Until recently Sandy would start a load of laundry on a Saturday afternoon. After getting the washer going in the garage, she would come into the house to tell me she was going out shopping for a while. I would say, "Great, honey, have a good time." She would respond, "Thanks, I will. See you later."

Sandy would leave and expect me to finish that load of laundry. The only problem was, *I had no idea* she even had clothes in the washer! How could I know that? She never said a word about it! Unless I happened to stumble into the garage and hear the washer, I would never have known.

Sandy would return home and say to me in a sarcastic tone, "Hey, thanks a lot for finishing the laundry for me."

"What laundry?" I would say with a straight face.

Sandy (I'm not kidding here) would actually think that I knew about the load of laundry and had selfishly ignored it. (Women!) I finally convinced her that she *has to tell me* about the laundry before she leaves if she *expects me to finish it* for her. Like most husbands, I am happy to meet a need as long as I am told what it is. If Sandy doesn't tell me, that is her fault, not mine.

I do try to focus on Sandy and anticipate some of her needs. If she leaves the house on Saturday without mentioning the laundry, I still run to the garage sometimes to check the washer. Sometimes there is a load going, and I can surprise her by finishing it. It is fun to meet one of her needs without her saying a word. But that is a very rare occurrence. The old saying "Even a blind squirrel finds a few acorns" comes to mind. You can't build a great, need-meeting marriage on those few times a year when a husband meets an unspoken need.

Tell your intimacy avoider in written form exactly what your basic, unchanging needs are. (Again refer to chapter 4 for a sample list of these "core" needs one wife wrote to her husband.) Also tell your IA verbally each day what you need. Be clear and specific. Do it every time. Follow these instructions, and your husband will have a decent chance to please you. And you will generate some genuine closeness.

The woman who talks too much

There is no delicate way to say it: You talk too much. You fill the air with words, tossing topic after topic after topic at your poor, overwhelmed husband. You don't even pause; you just keep on going as if you think conversation is like throwing spaghetti against the wall. Sooner or later something has to stick. I mean, one of these topics has to arouse his interest, right? He has to respond to something you say!

No, he doesn't. And most of the time he won't. He simply can't process all the sentences and paragraphs gushing out of your mouth. Your waves of words overwhelm his tiny brain, and it will explode. He shuts down. He gets distracted, tunes you out, and goes into the "zone," staring into the distance with no expression on his face. When you notice you have lost him, you will get upset. Conversation over. Actually there never was one. It was only you talking.

During those infrequent times he speaks, you don't let him finish. You interrupt, ask too many questions, demand more details, want him to clarify statements, and make too many observations. You cut in and ask him to share his emotional reaction to the events he is describing: "But, honey, how did that make you feel?"

You are driving him crazy. More importantly you are choking off any possibility he will keep talking and maybe get a little deeper. Your interruptions make him lose his train of thought. When you ask about his emotions, that is a question he literally

151

can't answer right then. He has no idea how he feels about what he is saying. He may be able to find some feelings about the topic a few hours (or a few days) later. But if you press him to identify his emotions on the spot, he will stop talking.

If you are in this "I talk too much" category, you will have to concentrate on reducing your flow of words. Talk less. Remember the two-minute rule for difficult messages I mentioned in chapter 10? For regular, no-conflict conversations, try the five-minute rule. Talk for five minutes with your husband and then stop. Give him a chance to think, digest what you said, and prepare some kind of response. He might say something back and he might not, but at least by pausing you give him an opportunity to engage with you.

If he says nothing during the pause, let a few minutes go by instead of jumping back in with more comments on the same topic. Discuss something else for five minutes, and pause again. If he doesn't respond, let ten or fifteen minutes pass. By being silent more often, you might motivate him to initiate more conversations. He will notice your silences (they are so rare!) and may talk more to draw you back closer to him.

Let him talk without interrupting. Don't worry, chances are he won't talk for long. When he finishes, give him your reactions and even ask a few questions. Say, "You don't have to respond right now. When you're ready, I would like to hear your answers to my questions." Give him time to process, dig down to a more personal level, and get back to you.

If you really want to hear back from him on a certain topic, whether you brought it up or he did, give him a reminder: "Remember that issue we discussed? When you're ready, please find me and tell me what you're thinking, and how you feel about that." Then drop it.

A Meeting of the Minds

The week is over. You are sitting face-to-face with your husband in the second meeting. Ask him to share the information he came up with in the three areas: his resentments against you, how you turn him away from conversation and intimacy, and what you can do to help him open up. Sit there with a pad and a pen. Write down everything he says.

If he gives you some solid input, do two things. First, thank him and promise him you will work hard to improve in the specific areas he mentioned. Second, tell him how you think you shut him down. Ask for his comments on your assessment of your role as his wife and work with him to create a list of new behaviors you will put into practice.

It is very likely that he will have little or nothing to say to you at this meeting. After all, he is an intimacy avoider and doesn't like to delve into personal matters. If he turns out to be less than a fountain of information, express your disappointment—again, using one-way communication—and schedule another meeting in two weeks. Do not share with him the ways you think you kill intimacy. Ask him to do the same assignment again and to come prepared in two weeks. Tell him you will now get input about your role as his wife from others who know you well.

Broaden the net

Don't just threaten to discuss this topic with others. Whether in person, by phone, or e-mail, contact your children, family members, and close friends and ask them to tell you how they think you push your husband away from intimacy. Make it clear this is very important to you and you must have the most honest, no-punches-pulled evaluations of your intimacy-killing behavior. Inform these individuals that you want to stop making mistakes, so you need their help to do it. Write down everything they communicate to you.

Catch me being good, catch me being bad

In the third meeting ask your husband for his report. When he finishes, share your own ideas and those supplied by outside sources. With his help (if he will give it), nail down the leading six or seven ways you stop conversations and closeness. Also identify the top six or seven ways you can motivate him to become intimate with you. Write these down and give him a copy.

Ask him to alert you to your conversation-stopping behaviors. Explain that you don't know when you take these negative actions and need him to tell you immediately. Ask your children, family members, and friends to also alert you when you are turning him off. Have your accountability partner ask you once a week if you have committed any of these relationship crimes.

Ask your husband and these individuals to catch you doing positive, intimacy-enhancing behaviors. Urge your husband to tell you every time he feels close to you and is willing to talk on a more personal level. If he will share this vital information with you, together you can pinpoint what you did to put him in this intimacy mode. If he doesn't provide this information, you will have to study his behavior yourself and try to come up with a list of things you did to nudge him closer to you.

STEP FIVE

THIS IS EXACTLY THE KIND OF WIFE I NEED TO BE

Chapter 12

God Says:
Be Submissive to Your Husband

A MERICAN CULTURE IS trying to help wives. Through television, movies, the Internet, newspapers, and magazines, our cultural "guides" have developed three distinct profiles of the twenty-first-century wife. As a public service I will describe American culture's three modern wives. Once you have read the descriptions, you can choose which wife you'd like to be.

The first prototype wife is glamorous and physically perfect. Her percentage of body fat is .001 percent. She is so thin, it is scary! She works out a minimum of fifteen hours per week on her NordicTrack, Stairmaster, and ThighMaster. And if physical exercise can't yield the body she wants, plastic surgery will. She fights the aging process with every technological advance known to medical science. She dresses in the finest designer clothes straight from Paris. Her makeup supply would make any supermodel shed jealous tears.

She worships at the altar of the Hollywood Actress Club, that special cadre of magically alluring women who believe they were placed on the earth to be beautiful and attract desirable men. Ironically this anorexically thin, surgically enhanced, botulism-injecting, liposuctioned babe will spend most of her life searching for the "right" man. She loves the intoxicating rush of infatuation and great sex. However, when the adrenaline surge of lust and excitement wears off—and it always does—she moves on to the next man. She remains convinced she will eventually find Mr. Perfect and he will make her happy. Surely he will make all her dreams come true.

The second modern wife hates men. All men. She sees men as chauvinistic, arrogant, insensitive, beer-guzzling, sex-crazed, nonexpressive, selfish dirtballs. Like radical feminists, she believes the path to true happiness is killing her husband and burying him in the backyard. She doesn't trust her husband, doesn't need him, and belittles him behind his back. She plans to get rid of him as soon as she can after he has fulfilled his role as a sperm donor. Her goal in life is to prove to everyone that she can make it just fine without a man.

The third choice our culture projects is the wife with a wildly successful career. She tries to get most of her needs met at work because that is where she spends most of her time. She plays hardball with the big business boys and always emerges on top. She gives her all to the company, has a corner office with a beautiful view, and is rich and powerful.

Incredibly this workaholic woman also has more than enough time and energy for her children and husband. She balances her roles of employee, mother, and wife in masterful fashion. Since her family understands her need to achieve, they are more than satisfied with the limited but quality attention they receive from her. She shows the world every day that a woman *really can* have it all!

Ignore the World, Listen to God

Ladies, if you attempt to embrace one of these culturally approved modern wives, you'll be personally unhappy and have a rotten marriage. American culture doesn't have a clue about what it takes to be a real wife. Who does? God. Throughout Scripture He speaks clearly to wives. His principles still apply, and if you obey them, you will have the best chance for a healthy, intimate marriage.

An important aspect of changing your intimacy avoider into the husband God wants him to be is being the wife God wants you to be. Not only does He know exactly what your husband needs from you, but He also doesn't hide this information. He spells it out in the Bible. To touch your husband's heart and shatter his IA shell, follow God's blueprint for a biblical wife:

- Be submissive.

- Be worthy of respect.

- Respect your husband.

It All Begins With Submission

Oh, no, the dreaded *S* word! For centuries submission has been one of the Bible's most misunderstood and misinterpreted marital teachings. Mere mention of the word can evoke intense, passionate reactions from both husbands and wives. Why? Because submission directly impacts every major area in marriage: balance of power, decision-making, personal safety and autonomy, communication, sex, finances, parenting... You can name any area of marriage, and submission is an integral part.

Wives, my goal in this chapter is to help you understand submission and to take specific steps to do what God wants you to do in this area. You need to be submissive to your husband because that is what God commands. So this is primarily an issue of obedience. However, it is also an issue of influence. When you submit to your husband, you are using a powerful and God-given tool to motivate him to love you and meet your real needs.

As we ought to always do, let's look again at a Scripture I cited earlier:

> Wives, be subject to your own husbands, as to the Lord. For the husband is the head of the wife, as Christ also is the head of the church, He Himself being the Savior of the body. But as the church is subject to Christ, so also the wives ought to be to their husbands in everything.
>
> —EPHESIANS 5:22–24

Scripture teaches that the husband is to be in the position of authority and leadership in the marriage relationship. Without a leader in any group of more than one you will have chaos. For reasons of His own God decreed that the husband is to lead his wife. Being the leader in a marriage is incredibly difficult. Being the one who submits and follows in a marriage is equally difficult. To help you submit in a healthy, biblical way, I will explain what submission does not mean and what it does mean.

Submission does not mean wives are inferior to husbands.

God created man and woman for each other (Gen. 1:27). The one-flesh relationship described in Genesis 2:24 is the ultimate picture of perfect unity. To be joined together as one, both must be equal.

In 1 Corinthians Paul asserts the complete equality of man and woman:

> However, in the Lord, neither is woman independent of man, nor is man independent of woman. For as the woman originates from the man, so also the man has his birth through the woman; and all things originate from God.
>
> —1 CORINTHIANS 11:11–12

Man and woman are to fit together in a God-designed, complementary way. Neither is independent of, or superior to, the other. This is a similar message as one that appears in a verse from Galatians, the most powerful and decisive statement possible on the equality of men and women:

160

> There is neither Jew nor Greek, there is neither slave nor free man, there is neither male nor female; for you are all one in Christ Jesus.
>
> —GALATIANS 3:28

We are all equal in Christ. Period.

Submission does not mean wives should keep quiet.

All too often wives are told that submitting means not expressing their opinions or feelings. This message is demeaning and insulting; it isn't even close to being biblical. It violates 1 Peter 3:7, which instructs husbands to treat wives with respect. Using submission to choke off a wife's right to expression contradicts a number of other biblical commands that we are to:

- "Be devoted to one another" (Rom. 12:10).

- "Accept one another" (Rom. 15:7).

- "Serve one another" (Gal. 5:13).

- "Bear one another's burdens" (Gal. 6:2).

- "Speak the truth in love" (Eph. 4:15, NLT).

Wives, feel free to talk and express yourself at any time (as if we could stop you). Actually many husbands try to do this, misusing a cultural interpretation of submission as their primary communication-killing method. And they are dead wrong!

Submission does not prohibit wives from having interests outside the home.

There are two mistakes commonly made in this area. The first holds the view that "a woman's place is in the home." The husbands who adhere to this position want their wives to focus solely on keeping house and taking care of their children, under the rallying cry: "Keep your wife barefoot and pregnant." Such men are stuck in a 1950s' time warp. Nor are they reading the same Bible I do. God does not want a wife just to be at home. If He did, we have to toss out the woman described in Proverbs 31.

The second mistake is society's view that every wife's number-one priority must be a successful career. In their eyes career always comes first. Then you can attend to your husband, children, and home duties. No, God doesn't think this way, either.

What *does* God teach in the Bible about the role of a wife inside and outside the home? He teaches *balance*. In Titus 2:4–5 God sends this message to wives through the apostle Paul:

> Older women likewise are to be reverent in their behavior, not malicious gossips, nor enslaved to much wine, teaching what is good, that they may encourage the young women to love their husbands, to love their children, to be sensible, pure, workers at home, kind, being subject to their own husbands, that the word of God may not be dishonored.

A married woman's primary place of responsibility is in the home. Meeting the needs of your husband and children ranks as your top priority, second only to your relationship with God. If your outside interests or your job cause your home duties to suffer, then you are violating Scripture.

Paul is clear about the priorities of a wife. Still, women are able to fulfill their biblical duties at home *and* be involved in other activities. In fact, all wives need outside activities and interests to keep from going stale or just plain crazy. Most husbands have no idea what it is like to be trapped at home all day...with children. Or to work outside the home and also have to do most of the housework. Ninety-nine percent of husbands wouldn't last a week doing what their wives do week in and week out, all year long. These husbands would become quivering, drooling, mumbling basket cases, shuttled off by ambulance or helicopter to the hospital for IVs, intensive therapy, and observation.

Take a look at the excellent wife of Proverbs 31. Even though she seems a little too good to be true, we can learn from her example. Her focus was undeniably on her household, but she did so many other things in her community:

> She considers a field and buys it; from her earnings she plants a vineyard.
> —PROVERBS 31:16

> She extends her hand to the poor, and she stretches out her hands to the needy.
> —PROVERBS 31:20

> She makes linen garments and sells them, and supplies the merchants with sashes.
> —PROVERBS 31:24, NIV

Does this sound like a wife who was chained to her home and didn't venture out into the big, bad world? Hardly. Proverbs 31:25 (NIV) is my favorite verse in this section of verses because it captures the essence of this remarkable woman:

> She is clothed with strength and dignity; she can laugh at the days to come.

Now that is a wife who made her husband sit up and take notice—a force to be reckoned with. She had significant influence in her man's life. She was one classy, impressive lady. She was confident, strong, productive, and happy. I am convinced a big reason is because she regularly ventured outside the home. Without a doubt her outside activities improved her household and benefited her family. They also provided healthy outlets for her creativity and self-expression.

If you are a married woman with preschool children, do not work outside the home unless it is absolutely necessary. Small children need their mom at home. Still, you must get some time out of the home each week—alone, without the kids. Inform your husband that if you don't get this time away, he will have one stressed-out, depressed, mean woman on his hands. Tell him, "It'll be continuous PMS, baby! When you look at a pit bull and me, the only difference will be the lipstick!" If he refuses to help you get away, enlist friends, family, neighbors, or fellow church members to stay with your kids. Do whatever you have to do to get regular mental health breaks from the home.

Back in the days when we had four young children rambling around our house, Sandy sat me down and told me she needed breaks from these little people every week. We worked out this deal and followed it for years: Sandy would get away from the home every Wednesday from 8:00 a.m. to noon, every Saturday from 9:00 a.m. to 1:00 p.m., and occasional evenings out with girlfriends. On the few days when I couldn't stay with the kids, we asked family or friends to help or hired a babysitter. If Sandy had had a particularly stressful day with the kiddos, she had the option of leaving for a few hours in the evening. She would meet me at the door when I came home from work and say, "They're all yours, buddy. I'm out of here!" Then she took off for the car and peeled off in a squeal of burning tires.

Wives, if you have to work outside the home, you have to work. God understands and He will help. He will protect your children. However, don't shoulder the domestic burden alone. Sit your husband down and tell him you need him to be the ultimate team player. Work out a contract that has him doing one-half of the chores and child-rearing duties. Inform him that if you have to work outside the home *and* do most of the household jobs too, you won't be a very good wife. You will be angry, hurt, and tired.

To make sure you get his attention, tell him if you are forced to carry the load at home, your sexual relationship will be a dud. Explain that when you feel exhausted and resentful, you won't be interested in sex. It will become just another chore. Sure, you will do it, but you won't be anywhere close to a warm, willing, or responsive partner. Go ahead and tell him what you are *really* thinking during sex after killing yourself all evening doing chores: "Are you through yet? Is it over? Please hurry up!"

Submission does not mean wives must tolerate abuse.

No, no, no. A thousand times no! You should not submit to physical or psychological abuse. Not ever. If your husband is abusing you, he is sinning in an extremely serious way, and God does not want you to submit to sin. God wants you to do just the opposite: stand up, confront him, and demand change (Matt. 18:15–17). I will discuss this in more detail in chapter 13.

What Submission Does Mean

Submission means to allow your husband to be the leader in your relationship and to yield to his authority. Not because he is superior, is more intelligent, or has more ability, but because this is the role God commands you to fulfill. Here is an explanation of how you can submit.

Walk close to God

You can submit to your husband only with God's power, through the Holy Spirit and Jesus Christ working in your life. If it is you, in your own power, trying to submit, you will never be able to do it. It is humanly impossible. It's a God thing. You must submit with God's help or you won't submit at all. (I already explained the importance of an intimate relationship with God in chapter 3.)

You also submit to your husband out of obedience to God. You don't submit for your husband. You submit for God:

> Wives, be subject to your own husbands, as to the Lord.
> —EPHESIANS 5:22

> Wives, be subject to your husbands, as is fitting in the Lord.
> —COLOSSIANS 3:18

As you submit, don't focus on your husband. Keep your eyes on the Lord; you are doing this for Him. He will bless you for your act of obedience and love.

As an equal partner, speak your mind freely

A critical part of your role as a submissive wife is to openly share your feelings and opinions on significant decisions and issues. Always. God wants you to offer your husband guidance and feedback:

> Then the LORD God said, "It is not good for the man to be alone; I will make him a helper suitable for him."
>
> —GENESIS 2:18

As a helper to your husband, you are to tell him in a loving, honest, and firm way what you think is best in every important situation. That is being helpful. If you remain silent when he is about to make a huge mistake, who else will correct him? Be like the Proverbs 31 wife:

> She opens her mouth in wisdom, and the teaching of kindness is on her tongue.
>
> —PROVERBS 31:26

Since you possess wisdom about your husband, children, and home that no one else does, you need to share it. While your husband may not always want to hear what you have to say, that is too bad. Lay it on him anyway. That is your job and part of submission.

Let Your Husband Lead

Allow your husband to make decisions in key areas of life and follow them unless they clearly violate God's revealed will. If you face a major decision, each of you can fully share your views about the situation and take time over several days (or several weeks) to decide. Pray about it together. Then, when your husband reaches a decision, you—whether you agree or not—should support him and his approach. Remember, he is accountable to God for his leadership, not you.

However, if he is actively sinning, you are not to submit. Instead, confront his sin and take action against it. If he asks you to do something that would break God's law, do not submit. Refuse to sin for him. Confront his sin and take action against it.

If he is harsh with your children, you must step in to protect them and confront his sin. If he is financially irresponsible, confront him and take steps to bring about repentance. If he says you can't go to church, go anyway. If he asks you to sign a fraudulent income tax form, refuse and confront that sin the Matthew 18 way.

The truth is, you can and should make many decisions on your own, such as child care, groceries and other purchases, many home-related areas, and your personal life. The Proverbs 31 wife did many things on her own for the good of her husband, children, and home. Still, in significant areas, the husband ought to chart the course and be responsible for making decisions.

Most of the time when the two of you talk issues through and pray about them, you will agree. However, sometimes you won't. When that happens, the husband must make the call. He is the leader. That's his job.

Over the twenty-nine years of our marriage, I have made some good decisions and some bad decisions. I mean, some real duds! The *what was I thinking?* type of decisions. Wives, please follow the example of my long-suffering wife, Sandy, and don't say, "I told you so!" That is not nice, and it's not submission.

What if he refuses to lead?

If your husband refuses to lead in a biblical way, submission becomes a moot point. You don't submit to him. Why? Two reasons.

1. There can't be submission if no leadership exists.

2. He is in violation of Scripture and is therefore sinning.

If your husband is not a leader, then *you* will have to lead the family. This is not God's plan A, but you have no other choice. You must lead family devotions, make sure home repairs get done, reach financial decisions, and guide your children's lives. If your husband crabs about your leadership, tell him you will step aside as soon as he assumes his God-ordained position as head of your marriage and family. Hopefully my Husband Transformation Strategy will help motivate and teach him to step up and be your leader.

Chapter 13

God Says:
Be Worthy of Respect

WHAT KIND OF woman does God want you to be? Outspoken and at the same time supportive, the woman who offers her husband the truth and love makes for an unbeatable combination. Examine the following examples and you'll get a clearer picture of what God is looking for in your life.

Now, That's a Woman!

- Sarah, who was so far past conventional child-bearing age it wasn't even funny, trusted God to give her a child. She assertively spoke her mind with her husband, Abraham, and remained at Abraham's side through many trials and painful circumstances.

- Miriam was tough enough to speak directly to Pharaoh's daughter and offer to get a nurse for her baby brother, Moses. That nurse was her—and Moses's—mother. Miriam helped lead Israel as a key aide to Moses.

- Rahab hid the Israelite spies, right under the noses of the Jericho authorities. Because of her faith in God and desire to protect her family, she risked everything.

- Abigail was a strong, intelligent woman who was married to the worthless, evil Nabal. She prevented the slaughter of her household by going behind her husband's back to supply provisions to David and his men. With clear, persuasive words, she convinced David to back away from violence. She not only helped God's man, but she also had the guts to tell Nabal what she had done.

- Deborah ruled Israel with wisdom, strength, and decisive action. She did not hesitate to tell her chief general, Barak, what she thought of his weak response to God's battle command. She went to war and brought peace to Israel for forty years.

- Ruth endured the loss of her husband and—refusing to stay in Moab—remained loyal to her mother-in-law, Naomi, and to God.

- Esther risked her life to stand against evil and save her people, the Jews. It wasn't her great beauty that defined her, but her character and her courage.

- Mary, the mother of Jesus, was caught in a crisis situation that was not her fault. Squeezed by tremendous pain and stress, she did the right thing. She did what God asked her to do and gave birth to the Savior and raised Him.

- Mary Magdalene loved Jesus with her whole heart. She didn't let her past sins or the criticism of others stop her from serving her Lord faithfully.

- Priscilla, the excellent wife of Aquila, was a prominent member of the early church and worked alongside the apostle Paul making tents. She also risked her life for Paul. And along with Aquila she confronted the orator, Apollos, and corrected his teaching.

Wow! These women were amazing, weren't they? Strong. Courageous. Assertive. Dignified. Women of character. Women of influence. Women of action. Women who were warriors in God's army. Women who spoke the truth without fear and without apology. Women who were willing to take a stand for themselves and for their God.

As I reviewed their stories in the Bible, it struck me that these dynamic women shared one essential quality: respect. They earned the respect of everyone who knew them, particularly the men in their lives. Such respect gave them the ability to influence others in positive, godly ways.

Likewise God wants you to have the kind of respect these biblical women possessed. When you have respect, you will have what it takes to implement my Husband Transformation Strategy. You will get your husband's attention and keep it, impact his life, and motivate him to change. And stay changed.

Be a 1 Timothy 3:11 Wife

First Timothy puts into words what these biblical heroines had and what God wants you to have:

> In the same way, their wives are to be women worthy of respect.
> —1 Timothy 3:11, niv

In this verse Paul was speaking to the wives of church leaders. Just as these wives needed respect to serve effectively in the local church, so all wives need respect to serve effectively in their marriages. Let's look at some practical ways you can be a wife worthy of respect.

Confront an Abusive Husband

Do not ever tolerate abuse from your husband. Ever. To allow yourself to be treated with such lack of respect is dangerous to you and your husband. You suffer a loss of dignity and emotional trauma. You will feel depressed, worthless, and be unable to carry out your biblical role in the home. By submitting to abuse, you are failing to give your husband the opportunity to stop the abusive behavior.

It is not God's will for you to allow behavior that harms you, your husband, your relationship, and your children. I recommend—and God requires—a strong, tough-love response to abuse. Abuse is sin and therefore must be confronted head-on the Matthew 18 way:

> If your brother sins, go and show him his fault in private; if he listens to you, you have won your brother. But if he does not listen to you, take one or two more with you, so that by the mouth of two or three witnesses every fact may be confirmed. If he refuses to listen to them, tell it to the church; and if he refuses to listen even to the church, let him be to you as a Gentile and a tax collector.
> —MATTHEW 18:15–17

If your husband has physically abused you in any way, such as hitting, kicking, or shoving, take your kids and leave the house—*immediately.* Call the police and take out a restraining order against him. Press charges of domestic violence and force him to face the full extent of the legal consequences of his actions. While I recognize this is easier said than done (especially if you fear for your life), believe me, you won't break the pattern of violence any other way. Staying with a man who has been physically violent is not only enabling him, but it is also dangerous.

If he is involved in an affair and refuses to stop when you confront him, get him out of the home. Kick him out! With the help of a few friends, pack up all his clothes and personal items in garbage bags. Call him at work and say, "Until you stop your affair, confess, repent, and prove real change, I don't want you living in this home. I have packed all your stuff; it's sitting in the driveway. Come and pick it up. You'd better hurry—it looks like rain."

Maybe your husband is psychologically abusing you. Are you living with an alcoholic? A man addicted to drugs? A man who flies into rages and screams at you and the kids? A man who regularly criticizes your weight, housekeeping, mothering skills, or other areas of your life? Shun this kind of a man. Don't talk to him. Don't have sex with him. Don't do his laundry, cook for him, or run errands for him.

You do not submit to sin and enable it. As God makes clear in Matthew 18:15–17, you are to resist sin. Confront it, fight it, and pull away from it. These biblical actions will protect you and your children. God doesn't want you to be destroyed by your husband's sin. In addition, your "tough love" may get his attention and motivate him to come to God and change

While God's goal is always restoration of the marital relationship, that can happen only if he changes. And as I have said throughout this book, he won't change unless he has to. When he realizes he has lost you, maybe he will break and do whatever it takes to win you back. If you do nothing, your husband won't suddenly wake up one day and change. You know what he will do? He will keep on abusing you until there is nothing left of you, the children, or the relationship.

Four Steps to Correction

Are you living with an abusive husband? If so, you need to take four steps:

1. Stand up and demand to be treated with respect.

If you are used to passivity, this may take a while. Get angry with a righteous anger (Eph. 4:26; Eccles. 3:5, 8) and stay angry until you have taken these four steps. It's amazing to me what some wives put up with from their husbands. I am saying—and I fervently believe God is saying—that you don't have to put up with it any more.

2. Pull back from the man emotionally and physically.

Stay back until he genuinely changes. Forget his promises. He has promised to change a million times and always returned to his sin, hasn't he? This time require consistent action over time. This time require Christian counseling and serious spiritual growth.

3. Follow the Matthew 18:15–17 steps.

Confront him one on one, then go back with one or two witnesses and confront him again. Next go to the leaders of your church and ask them to do an intervention. Finally, if he still refuses to repent and begin a program of change, shun him in your home. Ignore him and act as if he doesn't exist. If shunning doesn't work, then make plans to physically separate.

4. Reach out and get the support of family and friends.

You can't do this alone. It is too tough. Tell the secret. Tell your support team exactly what your husband is doing. When your supporters know, you get help and it will put pressure on the abuser. (For a complete, detailed description of how to apply Matthew 18:15–17 to a sinning spouse, read my book *What to Do When Your Spouse Says, I Don't Love You Anymore*.)

Steps to Respect

Even if your husband is just a basic intimacy avoider and not guilty of abuse, it is still important to be worthy of respect. You need to command respect as a wife. Without your husband's respect he may not abuse you, but he will mistreat you. He won't be attentive or open up and talk personally with you. He won't meet your needs. He won't love you the way you want and need to be loved.

When respect goes down, love deteriorates. If you behave like a doormat, the finest man in the world will wipe his feet on you. The crazy part is, he won't even know he is doing it! It is human nature!

Here are three ways to earn the respect of a nonabusive but still an IA husband:

Love yourself

God considers it important that you love yourself (Matt. 22:39). Base this love on God's love for you and a confidence founded in Him (2 Cor. 3:4–5). However, that can be difficult. There is an epidemic of poor self-esteem among American women. One reason is the nonstop cultural attack on women's self-image. If you are not an unbelievably thin glamour queen who juggles an amazing career with husband and kids with ease, society says you don't measure up; you are a failure. Wrong! The truth is, culture sets up a false, unrealistic standard. No woman, anywhere, can be that good. (Even the Proverbs 31 wife had her bad days.)

Another deeper reason for women's poor self-esteem is a poor relationship with their fathers. I see so many ladies in therapy struggling with a negative self-image. Ninety percent of these females have unresolved issues with their fathers. Ninety percent! That is the bad news. The good news is that 100 percent get better when they face the truth about the pain related to their father problems and work through them.

To learn how to love yourself, you first need to develop a close relationship with God and one other person. God gives you the power to change. A close female friend gives you human support, love, and accountability. Your relationship with God may be limited in some ways because your issues with your human father will transfer to your heavenly Father. Still, you can create a solid bond with God as you work—with His help—to heal from the pain your father caused.

With God and your close friend on your team (and, if necessary, a Christian therapist), you need to look honestly at the past. In fact, you will do more than look. You will relive your pain, losses, and what happened between you and your father. It will hurt—a lot. But it's also going to heal you. I will describe this process in more detail in chapter 15.

Get a life

To put it bluntly, every wife needs a life outside of her husband and family. While your husband and children are your priority, they are not everything! Go out and get a life. You are not just a wife or mother. You are a person! God has some valuable things for you to do outside your home.

In the first part of many marriages (including mine), the husband's career is the focus. It is all about him and how well he can do in his occupation. Your job is to support him, raise your children, and keep the home base healthy. This is normal and OK. The marriage and family need a solid financial and emotional foundation. However, in your thirties and forties, this approach needs to change.

Now, wives, it is your turn. You are still a good wife and mom, but you should start developing your own personal life. Build a deeper relationship with God. Use your spiritual gifts to serve in the local church. Cultivate a best friend of the same sex. Pursue a hobby or interest that *you* enjoy. This activity is yours and yours alone. Your husband may not like the interest you've chosen. Whatever! Remind him it's not about him. You may get involved at a nonprofit agency or parachurch group as a volunteer. You may go back to school. You may go out into the workplace and get a part- or full-time job.

My Sandy, who has passed fifty (she will kill me when she finds out I have written down her age), has spent the last ten years creating a life of her own. With all the kids finally in school, she has had the time to think of herself and do things just for her. I will never forget the day almost ten years ago when we dropped off our youngest child, William, for his first day at kindergarten. After shouting, screaming, and dancing around the parking lot for fifteen minutes, Sandy said to me, "Honey, you have no idea how happy I am right now. I love our kids, but I need a life. So look out, world, here I come." I said, "Go ahead, baby, you've earned it."

Sandy has built some fantastic friendships with several women in our church. They have breakfast together, walk in the mornings, talk on the phone, and go to the mall and movies together. Sandy also leads the middle school Sunday school class at our church. She loves serving as a camp counselor several weekends a year and two weeks in the summer. She sews up a storm. She cares for families who have special needs and is involved in evangelism. Sandy is still a terrific wife and mom, but she is also a healthy, developing individual.

Speak your mind

As I have already mentioned in detail earlier in this book, you need to always tell your husband the truth. You will do it in love (Eph. 4:15), but you will do it. Whenever your husband—whether he means to or not—treats you with a lack of respect, verbally point it out. If you are angry, hurt, offended, or insulted, go to him and tell him. Express the truth in the one-way communication style I described in chapter 10. Be brief. One or two sentences will get the job done.

The balance of respect is critical to your marriage. Telling your husband every time he crosses the line of respect will keep your system clean and you healthy. It will keep you from resenting him. Most importantly it will cause him to respect you. When he respects you, he will love you and treat you well. A man can truly love a woman he respects. She is his equal. She is a challenge. She has a powerful influence in his life. She can change him.

Chapter 14

=====

God Says:
Respect Your Husband

IF YOU WANT to know the best way to your husband's heart, read the Song of Solomon. If you want to learn how to motivate your husband to meet your deepest needs, read the Song of Solomon. If you want to be the wife God wants you to be, read the Song of Solomon. Study it, meditate on it, and embrace its message.

Solomon was the happiest husband in the world. He was ecstatic, thrilled, deeply satisfied, confident, safe, and secure. His book is called the *Song* of Solomon because he was whistling a happy tune. Why was he so joyful? One word: Shulamith.

Solomon's wife was an amazing woman. She knew exactly what she was doing as a wife. She made it her business to meet Solomon's needs. Attentive, affectionate, and incredibly complimentary. Solomon was her hero. This is what your husband needs to be—your hero!

Shulamith knew the secret to loving a man and connecting with him on the most intimate level. Her secret: she *respected* him. She realized that a husband's most important need is to be respected by his wife. The respect she had for Solomon drips from every page of this book. Shulamith respected him every day of their life together. She constantly lifted him up, praised his worth, and honored him for who he was and what he did. She made him feel like a real man.

What was the result of her respect for Solomon? What did he do in return? He loved her with a love so passionate, sensitive, and tender that it boggles the mind. I mean, when you read the Song of Solomon you just can't quite believe how loving Solomon was. You think: "Oh, please! He could not have been that fantastic a husband!" But he was. That's what the Bible says. Affectionate and focused on his wife's needs, Solomon showered her with all kinds of words and actions expressing his love. He treated her like a queen! Best of all he opened up and talked to her—and not just about the weather or the rusty wheels on his chariot. He shared personal, intimate things about himself, about her, and about their relationship. He gave himself to her.

Solomon did everything every wife wants her husband to do. What motivated him to be this kind of husband was the respect Shulamith gave him. That was her secret to getting the marriage partner of her dreams. You can do the same thing she did. I am going to show you how.

Peter, Paul, and Marriage

If the example of Shulamith isn't enough to convince you of the importance of respecting your husband, read the marital teachings of Peter and Paul. Both of these giants of the early church highlighted a husband's need to be respected by his wife.

Peter makes the point that husbands can be changed by their wives, even come to faith in Christ "as they observe your chaste and respectful behavior" (1 Pet. 3:2). Just a few verses later he continues and expands on his instruction:

> Just as Sarah obeyed Abraham, calling him lord, and you have become her children if you do what is right without being frightened by any fear.
> —1 Peter 3:6

179

In case you were wondering, you don't have to call your husband, "Lord." He would probably love it, but that is going a little too far. Still, God wants you to give your husband the kind of respect Sarah gave Abraham, recognizing him as the leader of their marriage and family.

Paul concludes his powerful section on marriage in the fifth chapter of Ephesians with this final charge for husbands and wives:

> Nevertheless, each individual among you also is to love his own wife even as himself, and the wife must see to it that she respect her husband.
>
> —EPHESIANS 5:33

As Paul drives home so clearly in that last line, there is nothing a wife can do that is more important than respect her husband. You must treat him as someone who is important and worthy, whom you admire, and who impresses you.

Remember, God commands that you respect your husband. It is not an option. This is a lifestyle. Your respect will meet one of his deepest needs as a man and as a husband. And when he feels respected by you, he is much more likely to make the changes you want him to make. Isn't that your ultimate goal?

How do you respect your husband? You follow the three Ps.

1. Praise him

Men literally thrive on praise. It is our lifeblood. It is what gives us energy, confidence, power, and passion. Have you ever seen your husband and a group of his male friends watching a football or basketball game together? Or playing a sport? There is constant praise and encouragement flying around, right? "Way to go," "Atta boy," "Great shot," "That was sweet," and other expressions of positive reinforcement flow freely and often. Guys are always back slapping, fist hitting, and high-fiving each other.

Your husband needs approval and encouragement, and he needs it from *you*. If Sandy doesn't praise me on a regular basis, I don't feel loved by her. She can do all kinds of things for me, but without her praise I feel insecure and discouraged. I think she's not impressed with me and what I'm doing at work and in the home. As a result, I get quieter and withdraw. Sound familiar?

If you want to deflate your husband's ego and drive him away from you, just continue to not praise him. I say continue because I am willing to bet that you are not very good at praising him. You tend to notice all the things he *doesn't* do, don't you? And you point out these mistakes to him, don't you? You overlook all the positive things he does do for you and the family, don't you?

Your husband needs praise in the same way you need personal talk and emotional connections. If you think you are already praising him enough, you'd better make sure. Ask him how you are doing in the praise department. Whatever he says, concentrate on praising him as much as you can. You can't praise him too much. You do have to be honest with him about his mistakes, but at the same time you had better be praising him for what he's doing right.

Earlier in my Husband Transformation Strategy I urged you to not praise your husband. At this point in my strategy it's time to start praising him.

Compliment him often, using Shulamith as your example. She was very flattering to Solomon. I mean, it's almost sickening to read the many sweet things she showered on him, like the following description:

> My beloved is like a gazelle or a young stag.
> —SONG OF SOLOMON 2:9

"Young stag" was one of Shulamith's favorite pet names for Solomon; she repeats it in Song of Solomon 2:17 and 8:14. In today's language *stag* means *stud*. Once or twice a week when your husband comes home from work, say, "How are you, stud?" He is a stud! (After all, he is the only stud you have.) I guarantee you, he will like that. Tell him he's handsome, charming, or an outstanding worker and family man. Comment positively on his character and integrity. Tell him he looks sharp in his khaki pants and blue blazer. Mention that he is one of the few men you know who makes a real effort to keep his nose hairs clipped. Whatever. You get the idea. Just compliment him on a regular basis.

Thank him for working at his job. Nobody thanks him for doing that job. He needs you to thank him, at least once a week. Thank him for the chores—no matter how few—that he does around the house. Thank him for behavior you like. The next time he takes out the trash, run down the driveway and high-five him: "Give me five, baby; way to go with that trash!" Then slap him on the bottom and say in a loud voice so the neighbors can hear: "You are the trash man!"

The next time he unloads the dishwasher, act like it is *a big honking deal*! Say something nice and positive to him. You will likely be thinking: "Big whoopee! I've unloaded that thing the last 899 times. He'll probably put the dishes away in the wrong spots anyway." Hold your tongue! Instead say, "Thank you, young stag. That's an outstanding job! You are the dishwasher-unloading man!"

Have you noticed your husband fishing for compliments and praise? He will do some small job and mention it to you:

- "Hey, I put gas in your car."
- "I did a load of laundry for you."
- "I took out that big, smelly garbage bag."
- "How does the yard look?"

If he is fishing, you are not doing your job. Don't make him beg for your praise. Give it to him all the time. If you don't praise him, he will assume you don't care about the job he did. He'll assume you don't care about him. He will assume he can't ever please you and that you don't love him.

If you do praise him regularly, you will kill three birds with one stone: 1) he will continue the behavior you praised and do even more, hoping for additional praise; 2) he will feel loved; 3) and best of all, your praise will help motivate him to become a better husband. Your praise gives him confidence and security. Your praise makes him feel closer to you, gives you more influence in his life, and motivates him to try and please you in the areas most important to you—spirituality, communication, needs, romance, and leadership. So start praising your husband and never stop.

Play with him

On just about every survey taken by a sample of husbands— anywhere in the world—the number-one thing they want from their wives is more sex. No shocker there. The number two need, however, usually comes as quite a surprise to most women: husbands wish they and their wives did more enjoyable activities together. Shared activities and interests are the heart's desire of nearly every husband. Your husband wants to spend time with you doing something fun like a sport or hobby:

- "Honey, let's play golf."
- "Let's go fishing."
- "Let's play tennis."
- "Let's go to the football game (or baseball game, basketball game, or NASCAR race)."
- "Let's watch this sporting event or action-adventure movie on television."
- "Let's go visit eighty-five stores at the mall while I watch you try on and talk about two thousand articles of clothing but not actually buy anything."

OK, I'm kidding about the mall. He wants you to do things *he* enjoys, not what *you* enjoy. Hopefully as he transitions from intimacy avoider to sensitive husband he will also do activities you find entertaining. But hey, don't ask for that up front. Start with *his* activities. Besides, this section is about *his* needs, not *yours*. He will love it when you join him in his leisure-time pursuits. One backdoor way to eventually get him to join you in your world of communication and emotional connection is to first join him in his.

When you are doing something he likes to do, it relaxes him and puts him at ease. Feeling respected and happy, he is much more likely to lower his traditional male defensive guard. When he is more open, it increases the chances he will talk on a deeper level. Pursue such connections, and you may find bridges forming between you that aren't there at any other time in your relationship.

Men have trouble talking personally when they're just sitting around doing nothing. Men talk and express when they're in action or viewing something that holds their attention. If your husband is having fun while engaging in one of his interests, he will feel closer to you, creating a mood conducive to conversation. His tongue will be loosened, and some personal, revealing statements may slip out. Absent activity, with you just staring at him, *waiting* for him to say something, he has a terrible time talking. However, when he focuses on an interesting activity and talking isn't expected, he talks! He will say personal things to you during playtimes that he would never, ever say sitting with you in the den or at a restaurant.

You may be able to cut some deals with your husband, using your involvement in his interests as a bargaining chip. Men are essentially fair-minded creatures and understand deals—it is the "I'll scratch your back and you'll scratch mine" principle in action. If he doesn't share personally during a shared activity, say, "Honey, I did _____ with you, and I enjoyed being with you. Now,

I'd like you to take me out Friday evening for a romantic dinner so you can talk to me about your job, the stress you've been under, and where we're going as a couple." Men don't like surprises, so give him the agenda. That way he can make some notes in advance. He might not go for this kind of deal. But because you met his need by spending playtime with him, he might.

Pursue him sexually

If there are any men reading this far into the book, you're thinking, "Yes, yes, yes, yes, yes! Now you're talking my language." Almost all husbands dream—literally dream—that someday their wives will be more interested in sex. I can virtually guarantee that your husband wants more sex. And he especially wants you to be more excited about sex. He wants you to want him physically. There is nothing as invigorating and stimulating as your woman wanting your body.

I have made a shocking breakthrough in my research: physical affection and sex are important to men. It is a God-given need. That's right, ladies. We need sex, and if we don't get it...we will die! Please, save our lives! Read Song of Solomon, and you'll be amazed at how Shulamith was all over Solomon. Not only was she attracted to his body, she let him know it—often. She couldn't keep her hands off him. Solomon loved every minute of it. He loved her for pursuing him physically.

Most men crave their wives becoming more aggressive in the physical area. Your husband may not admit it, but always being the initiator gets old. Very old. Walking down the hall begging and pleading. Tugging at your skirt. Instead, come to us, please. Touch us. Put your hands on us. Make us feel like men!

Ladies, you know how to do this. Your husband's sitting on the couch, watching television or staring off into space. For once there are no kids in sight. You go into the bedroom and slip into something "more comfortable." You spritz on some perfume, like "Sensuality Under the Palms" or "You Wild Thing." You glide down the hallway in your slinky outfit, sit down next to him, cross your legs the way you do, and then in a soft, sultry voice say: "Hey, big boy! New in town?"

He won't be able to shut the remote off fast enough! Even if it is the last twenty seconds of the big game and the score is tied...he will turn it off without a second thought. You are there, looking good, and you want him.

You don't have to initiate affection and sex all the time. How about once a week or once every two weeks? Could you? Wives say to me: "Oh, I can't do this. It's too embarrassing. I'm too conservative."

"Get over it, you prude," I reply.

You don't come on to him in front of the neighbors or the kids! Just when it is you and him. Believe me, he will absolutely love it. He'll feel like a young stag, like he's still *got it*. He will feel respected in the best possible way—the way that God wants you to offer it to your spouse. Your stag. Your stud. Your hero.

STEP SIX

I NEED YOUR HELP
TO HEAL FROM
MY PAST PAIN

Chapter 15

How to Sneak
Inside Your Husband

R EMEMBER THE STORY of the Trojan horse? The Greeks and Trojans were locked in a ten-year war with no end in sight. The mighty walled city of Troy was impregnable. The Greeks simply could not break through the massive, thick walls that the Trojans had built around their city.

Finally the Greeks came up with a brilliant strategy. They built a large, hollow wooden horse, filled it with Greek soldiers, and left it outside the gates of Troy. They pretended to withdraw their army. The Trojans, thinking the war was over, brought the horse inside the city. They thought it was some kind of gift.

But that night the soldiers hiding inside the horse climbed out and opened the gates of Troy to the waiting Greek army. The city was completely destroyed and the Greeks won the war.

You Need a Trojan Horse

Your husband is a lot like the ancient fortress of Troy. Over the years he has built huge, impenetrable walls around his heart. He has literally walled off his personal life from everyone, including you. He won't let you inside. You have tried everything to break through and get to know the real him, but with no success.

What you need is a Trojan horse to sneak inside. You want him to bring you inside his walls without him realizing it. Unlike the Greeks, though, your goal is not to destroy your husband but

189

to persuade him to open up, talk personally, and connect with you emotionally. But you have to get inside to reach that goal.

Steps one through five of my Husband Transformation Strategy are crucial and need to be done in that specific order. Hopefully they will soften up your intimacy avoider's defenses and bring progress in your communication campaign. Now it is time for the final push in your offensive. Step six is your Trojan horse. You will tell your husband, "I need your help to heal from my past pain." This will be the decisive strike to sneak inside his heart and mind.

Dredge Up Your Past Pain

What I want you to do is spell out for your husband—in intimate detail—all the significant pain you experienced before meeting him. You are going to write letters to every person in your past that caused you serious pain. I know you can remember at least several individuals who did or said something that harmed you. Something that tore your heart up and left a scar. As you read these words, you are likely picturing in your mind's eye those individuals who traumatized you in some way, aren't you? You know who they are—you haven't forgotten them or what they did. You may have tried to forget, but the pain is still inside. It is time for the pain to come out.

Maybe your mother hurt you, or your father. A brother or a sister. A cousin. An aunt or uncle. A grandparent. A stepfather or stepmother. A foster parent. A neighbor. A teacher. A coach. A Sunday school teacher or youth leader. A pastor. A boyfriend or girlfriend. A close friend. A fiancé. An ex-spouse. A child. A boss. A fellow employee.

In addition to feeling angry and hurt because of what others did to you, you probably have done things that *you* regret. Things that you're ashamed of or did damage to you and close friends or family members. Drinking. Drugs. Premarital sex. Lying.

Gossiping. An abortion. Gambling. Overspending. An eating disorder. Divorcing someone without biblical grounds. Treating one of your children harshly. Jealousy. An explosive temper. We all have sinned. What are yours?

Not only do I want you to write letters to those who have hurt you, but I also want you to write letters confessing your sins and apologizing to those *you* have hurt. These letters will be the complete, honest truth in living color. Cover all the details; don't leave anything out. These heartfelt expressions of the pain you experienced, or inflicted on others, will be raw, ragged, and intense. You will not spare those who hurt you, or yourself, from responsibility. You will not use excuses or rationalize anything. Just share the stories and the pain attached to them.

Pray before you write each letter, asking God to bring forth the memories and pain that needs to get healed. Pray that He will guide, strengthen, comfort you, and give you the ability to forgive. Before you start wondering how I can suggest completing such a bone-jarring, fear-inducing exercise, let me add that these letters are not to send—only to read to your husband. Later you may want to read them to a therapist and a close friend. And you may choose, with God's direction, to send "cleaned up" versions of these letters to certain individuals.

I want you to write these letters even if you have already resolved your past pain with the help of a therapist. If you didn't include your husband in the process, then you missed a step. *You* may have found healing while overlooking a golden opportunity to change your husband and your marriage. Walking through such a personal journey with your husband can get you inside his walls, leading to a breakthrough in communication and intimate connections.

I am asking you to do something that is extremely difficult. I understand that. After leading many couples through this kind of process, I have seen up close and personal how emotionally demanding it is. You will relive the worst times in your life and allow your husband to see it and feel it with you. It requires considerable vulnerability and carries the risk of him not responding or opening his emotional gates to you. I believe it is a risk worth taking. The benefits of letting him see and feel your pain far outweigh the potential pain of disappointment should he choose not to respond.

Check Out the Benefits

You will heal from the pain.

The pain is still inside, and it is affecting every area of your life. In chapters 9 and 10 I explained the importance of forgiving your husband for all the ways he has hurt you. Now you need to forgive all the other people who have hurt you. When you do that, you will be healthier physically, emotionally, and spiritually.

You will be a better wife because you won't transfer your pain to your husband.

Though unintentional, certain words and behaviors of your husband will trigger memories of the unresolved pain caused by other people. When that happens, your past pain will shoot out of you like a white-hot laser beam, striking your husband. Suddenly your husband is not just receiving your anger and hurt for whatever he did, but he's also catching it for what *others* have done to you. Once you and he have worked through your past pain together, such transfers are less likely to occur. He won't unknowingly trigger such pain, and you will be able to deal with current issues instead of getting stuck in the past.

You and your husband will be closer.

Sharing your pain with your husband will bring the two of you closer in a way you've never known before. Doing this kind of deep emotional work will automatically propel your relationship to a deeper level; there is an intimacy in shared pain that cannot be found in any other experience.

Your husband will learn critical communication skills.

As you express your pain through reading these letters and in follow-up conversations, he will learn how to better listen to you, reflect, and build understanding. He will learn—probably for the first time in his life—what it feels like to connect with someone on a deeper level. When he reaches such depths consistently by helping you heal, it will be easier for him to reach intimate levels with you during many other conversations. Once he knows how, he knows how—and can do it repeatedly.

When he connects to your pain, he has a chance to connect to his.

You are not the only spouse here with unresolved pain. Chances are he has plenty of pain in his past too. He just walled himself off from it. In fact, he likely has walled himself off from almost all deeper emotions. However, dealing with your pain will energize his emotional system. With the wheels finally turning, there is a good chance your past pain will trigger his past pain. Because he is getting used to feeling your pain, he may be able to feel his and share it with you.

You will be able to say you gave it your best shot.

Regardless of what happens in the future, it is crucial that you believe you have done everything possible to improve your marriage. You don't want any regrets. You don't want to look back over the years of your marriage and realize that all you did was wait, hope, and pray as your spirit withered away more each day. If all you did was tough it out in silent misery, you didn't do much! When you share your pain with your husband in the way I'm about to describe, you will know with certainty that you did everything you could to change your husband.

"Honey, Here's What I Need From You"

Tell your husband you want to set up another meeting. He will instantly think (he might even blurt it out), "Oh, no, not another meeting!" But you should respond: "Yes, dear, another meeting. Marriage is just a series of meetings." Schedule the meeting and let him know it will be about something vitally important and extremely personal to you.

Start the meeting by taking his hands in yours and praying. Pray these words, or something similar:

> *Dear Father,*
>
> *I'm scared right now. I have something very important to ask my husband, _____, and I don't know how he's going to respond. I have some painful work to do on myself, and I need Your help and his help to do it. Father, give me the courage to ask for his help and to do the work I have to do. Dear Lord, please open his heart so he will help me through what I have to do. This will be very tough for both of us, so please give us strength and guidance through this process. Amen.*

OK, you have his attention. He is wondering what is coming next. Here's what you say (again, adapt the words to fit the way you would say them):

> Honey, part of Dr. Clarke's strategy for improving our marriage is for me to work through painful things that have happened to me in the past. There are people who really hurt me, and I've never completely healed from those hurts. As you know, you are one of those people. I have already cleaned out the anger, resentment, and hurt that you caused. I've forgiven you and will keep on expressing directly to you new pain you cause me, so I can continue to forgive you.
>
> But there are other people in my past—before I met

you—who hurt me deeply. Plus I have done things to hurt others. These unresolved hurts are still inside me and are damaging me physically, emotionally, and spiritually. My unresolved pain takes a toll on our marriage. When you do things—usually unintentionally—that remind me of how others have hurt me, it triggers my past pain and I over-react. I get too angry, too intense, and too upset. I know that pushes you away.

Now it's time for me to clean out all my pain from the past and forgive. I need to forgive those who hurt me and feel forgiven for the mistakes I made to hurt others.

Honey, I can't do this difficult work alone. Of course I'll have God on my side. But I need someone I know and trust to walk alongside me as I face and express my past pain. This has to be someone who loves me very much and wants the best for me. This has to be someone who is willing to sacrifice time and energy to be my partner in healing. Honey, I want you to be that person. Before you answer yes or no, here are the steps I'll be taking and what I need you to do.

I will write letters to those from my past who caused me significant pain. I will also write letters to those whom I feel I hurt with my actions. These letters will be raw, ragged, and detailed. The intensity and pain I express will prob-ably shock you. *I won't be sending these letters.* I'll just read them to you. I need you to listen as I read. I need you to reflect back to me what I'm saying and how I'm feeling. Don't just listen in silence. Tell me what you are sensing about the basic content and my emotions.

Do your best to feel some of the pain I'll be feeling. Share my pain. Please try to relive my pain with me. I'll tell you what I need as I'm reading, so you won't have to guess if you're on the right track.

After I read each letter, I will need a number of follow-up talks with you to vent the pain and process the stuff I put in the letter. These talks will last about fifteen to twenty minutes. I'll want at least two of them per week. I'll need to talk about the pain until the intensity of it lessens and I feel like I've settled it in my heart and mind. I'll go over the same details I put in the letter. I'll probably bring up other details that weren't in the letter. I'll yell and cry. I'll ask why these things happened. Sometimes I'll just be quiet and want you to hold me.

Honey, I need you to listen and reflect during these follow-up talks. Just as you did during the reading of the letter, let me know that you are trying to understand and feel the pain I'm feeling. Tell me what I'm saying and what you think I'm feeling. Ask me questions. If I'm angry, try to feel angry. If I'm sad and hurt, try to be sad and hurt. I know you're not good at this; just show me you're trying. I can heal more completely and quickly when you and I are facing and feeling this pain together.

In these talks I'll also tell you how I think my pain transfers to you and our marriage. I'll ask you to give me your input on what I'm doing: how *you* think my pain transfers to our marriage, how you see the pain affecting my life, any insights into me that you discover as you listen to my pain, and any ways my pain is triggering your pain from your past. I'll give you time between these talks to think and process any responses you might have. I know you can't give your input right away, but I absolutely have to have you listen and reflect. It's not essential, but I'd also love to get your input and reactions in these areas I just mentioned.

Dr. Clarke says this process—the letters and the follow-up talks—can take two to three months or even longer. Believe me, this is not all we'll be doing. We'll still keep our marriage going in all other areas. But I am convinced that working with you on my pain will heal me. I'll be a healthier person and a better wife. I also think it can bring us closer as a couple. Would you help me in this process? Would you be my partner in healing my past pain?

Tell him he doesn't have to give you an answer right away. Tell him you know this is a lot to take in and ask if he has any questions. If he isn't shocked into total silence, he will have some questions. Since you've written down on paper what you just said, give him the letter at this time. He may need to read it as he decides what to do. If he agrees to help you, he will need to reread this orientation letter frequently to remind him what you need him to do in this process.

Your husband will almost certainly say yes. He may not be sure exactly what he is getting into, but he will say yes. He is a good guy. He loves you, so he will want to help you. If for some reason he says no, he is not a good guy. He is a selfish guy and is sinning. I recommend three things:

1. Use one-way communication to express to him your feelings of anger, rejection, and deep hurt.

2. Write the letters and follow-up talks without his involvement, using a Christian therapist and a close, same-sex friend to help you work through your past pain. At least you will be a healthier person at the end of the process.

3. Read and apply the biblical, tough love approach I will explain in chapter 17.

Some of you reading this may not have trauma in your past. Your home was solid and safe, you had great parents, and your life prior to marriage ran pretty smoothly. You still need to go through this process because it has the power to change your marriage. Go with the pain you do remember. No one has experienced a pain-free life. Dredge up whatever you can.

A Walk Through

Let me walk you through the process so you know what to do. When you have finished writing your first letter, schedule the reading for a Friday or Saturday. Give yourself adequate time to read the entire letter. You will need at least a half-hour to forty-five minutes. You must read the letter in a quiet, private place at home. No distractions allowed. Make sure the kids are in bed or occupied. No television. You won't answer the phone or go to the front door. Read it in a comfortable setting, such as your family room or den. Make sure the lighting is low so your man has a better chance to respond emotionally in a casual, warm atmosphere.

Before you read the letter

Take his hands in yours and pray that God will be with both of you. Ask Him to help you heal and help your husband listen and understand your pain. Ideally, both of you will pray; if your husband won't, you should. After prayer ask your husband to do his best to reflect what you say and feel as you read the letter. Tell him it is OK to interrupt when he wants to offer statements of reflection or encouragement.

As you read

Pause every few paragraphs and give your husband a chance to reflect and build understanding. When you pause, ask him to tell you what you just said and how he thinks you are feeling. He needs these prompts because when it comes to intimate conversation, IAs don't know what they are doing. This process is one of the best ways he can learn. The truth is, he's in emotional connection and communication school, and you are the professor. Make sure you tell him repeatedly that you want his reflection and understanding because it helps you heal. He will work on these critical skills for *you*, to help *you*. At the same time he is learning tools that will transform him and your marriage. (He doesn't have to know about the school part yet.)

If he catches on to the education strategy, simply say: "Honey, first and foremost I need you to reflect and share my pain, because that will help me forgive and leave all this misery behind. Secondarily, as you get better at emotionally connecting with me, our marriage will be better. So, yes, both are true."

After reading

Thank him for listening and trying to feel your pain. Praise his effort. Husbands need praise, remember? Hand him a copy of the letter only after you are done reading the letter, and ask him to reread it several times. Ask him to pray about your pain, think about it, and process it. Ask him to work hard to feel it and respond to it. Tell him you would like to know such things as his observations, insights, what he has learned about you, how he sees your pain affecting your marriage, and what pain in his life your letter triggered.

It's a good idea to pray with him again after reading the letter. In your prayer thank God for a husband who is willing to do this with you. Ask God to help your husband process your pain and respond to it.

Finally, schedule the follow-up meetings. You need to have at least two follow-ups a week to keep the pain fresh and your husband engaged. Leave a few days between meetings to allow sufficient time for each of you to process. I recommend Monday and Thursday for these meetings. They will be fifteen to twenty minutes long—any longer and your husband will get distracted and overwhelmed. Sometimes, if you are both getting into it and he's OK with continuing, you can go longer. How many follow-ups? At least four and maybe even six. You need this many to vent, process, and heal. Your husband needs this many to practice emotionally connecting with you.

In follow-up meetings

Begin with prayer, asking God to be with you as you work together and that the Holy Spirit would bring any memories or thoughts to mind that you might have overlooked. As with the first session choose a quiet, private place where you can screen out all distractions.

After prayer ask your husband if he has any responses to share. At the second meeting ask if he has anything to share about your first letter. As you progress, he may have comments about previous letters or follow-up meetings. If he shares, great. Reflect what he says and interact with him about his statements. If he says nothing—which will likely be the case early in the process—move into verbally processing the latest letter. Vent your feelings, thoughts, and pain. Tell him any additional memories, details, and insights God has brought to mind in the past few days.

As you express yourself in these follow-up meetings, pause occasionally (just as you did as you were reading your original letter) and ask your husband to reflect and understand your pain. Give him the words and phrases to use because he won't know what to say.

At the close of each follow-up meeting, pray again. Ask God to continue helping each of you process the pain. Afterward thank your husband for spending time with you and trying to help you in the healing process. Ask him to pray and process before the next meeting.

Follow this same procedure until you've expressed all the significant pain from your past. You write a letter, read it, have follow-up meetings, and then write another letter. This will prove challenging for both of you and require faith and perseverance. It will hurt. But it has the potential to change your husband. It has the potential to give him a taste of the emotional intimacy he has been missing his whole life. It has the potential to give you the emotional intimacy with your husband that to now has been missing from your marriage.

Around the fourth or fifth follow-up meeting, or whenever you sense you are nearing the end of each cycle of letter and follow-ups, ask your husband to write a letter to you summarizing the process. Ask him to outline what you have shared, your feelings, and his responses to your pain. Tell him to do his best and not worry about being right or wrong. Tell him you just want a heart-felt response. Ask him to do it for you. Make it clear that hearing him read this kind of letter will promote your healing. If he will do it, it will also help him reach a deeper level in his emotional life and in his relationship with you.

To make certain that you understand and can apply step six, I am going to show you how it works in real life. In the next chapter I will describe one couple's journey through the process of healing together from past pain.

Chapter 16

From Superficial
to Super Husband

R AY WAS A classic intimacy avoider. In fact, he was more
than that. He was a Super IA. A world class IA. When we
first met, I actually thought he was a cyborg. You know,
one of those machines engineered to look and act like humans
that you can watch on old *Star Trek* episodes.

The man was emotionally flat. From an early age he had
learned to stuff his emotions deep down inside. He spoke in a
monotone and rarely laughed or smiled. To him, life and marriage were serious business. He showed passion only during sex
or when he was watching a ball game on television. He was a
good, solid, and moral man, but he was also a boring, life-sucking,
stress-inducing, and unbelievably frustrating man to live with.

Ray learned the IA trade from his father—a rigid, unemotional creature of habit who followed the same routine for forty
years: up at 5:15 a.m., read the paper and eat a bagel, work until
6:00 p.m., dinner at 6:30 p.m., finish reading the paper by 7:30
p.m., watch television until ten o'clock, and sip a cup of hot tea
before going to bed at 10:15 p.m.. Ray's dad didn't drink, do drugs,
smoke, gamble, or womanize. He also didn't talk personally,
reveal himself in any way, express love verbally, or provide any
physical affection. He also didn't realize what a lousy husband
and father he was.

Ray's mother did nothing to change the IA she married. Ray

saw his mother tolerate his dad's anti-intimacy behavior year after year. Mom seemed happy enough with his dad. She never complained, raised her voice, or asked for anything. She bravely took care of the home and kids, supported her husband as best she could, and carried on with a brave smile and grim determination to finish the race.

Ray's wife, Susie, was a bright, funny, spontaneous, and emotionally expressive woman. She was also getting tired of life with Ray. She still loved him but told me living with an intimacy avoider was getting old. Very old. Susie longed for Ray to open up and let her into his inner world. She desperately wanted and needed Ray to express his personal thoughts and emotions to her.

She tried everything she could think of to deepen their intimacy and emotional connection between them but had failed miserably. Nothing motivated Ray. Like all IAs, he was a master at avoiding intimacy and making her feel guilty for wanting more out of their marriage. Like all IAs, he was convinced they had the best possible marriage. She knew that wasn't true and that they could go much deeper in many areas. She thought she couldn't do anything about it.

In addition to the pain of an emotionally unfulfilling marriage, Susie carried a lot of pain from her past. Her father was a rigid, unaffectionate, and largely absent IA. While she loved her dad and wanted to know him on a deeper level, that never happened. As a young woman she searched for love and attention in the arms of a series of selfish, worthless men. She was also holding onto a tremendous amount of guilt and shame for the abortion she had in her late teens. Her first husband was an abusive, narcissistic, emotionally unavailable womanizer.

When I met Susie, she struggled with depression and low self-esteem. So far in her life no man had ever genuinely loved her and met her deepest needs. She believed that would never happen. She wondered if there was anything she could do to change her husband and her marriage. I told her there was quite a bit she could do. I explained my Husband Transformation Strategy and convinced her to give it a shot. Though not optimistic, she agreed to give it a try.

The Opening Salvos

Step one

Susie put her support team in place. She grew closer to God, developed a small group of two close female friends (also married to IAs), and remained active in her local church. She and her friends prayed for change in their husbands and gave each other support, encouragement, and accountability.

Step two

At her request Ray read chapters 5, 6, and 7 on how to be a biblical husband. The material proved to be a real eye-opener, helping him realize he fell well short of God's standards for a husband. He told her he wasn't sure he could do it all. Susie assured him that, with God's help, together they could get him to where God wanted him to be.

Susie read her letter to Ray detailing her needs. He was blown away. He felt bad that he hadn't been meeting her most important needs, and she let him feel bad. Since he felt overwhelmed and unsure of where to begin, she asked that he take three specific actions: 1) initiate a thirty-minute talk each evening, 2) lead a brief, joint prayer session three times a week, and 3) initiate a monthly marriage evaluation.

Step three

When Susie read her letter of resentments to Ray, it shocked him to the core. After a few days of defensiveness, he realized how tough he had been on her over the years. He started to "get it." He apologized for the pain he had caused and promised to change over time. Susie continued to vent about the past until she felt completely cleansed.

Through one-way communication Susie told Ray *whenever* he did or said something that significantly bothered her. Ray couldn't revert to his old habits, because Susie continually kept him off-balance. Her brief, honest comments helped him focus on his weaknesses and interrupted his marriage-killing behaviors.

Susie's regular honesty improved their communication. She learned how to speak the truth without her typical, high-voltage anger and intensity. Ray learned how to listen better, take time to process what Susie had said, and respond.

Step four

When Susie asked him to tell her what she did to kill intimacy, Ray had no response. But after a few weeks he told her some things she needed to know. He admitted he had been harboring resentment at her for years over two events in their past: her unwillingness to reach out and build a decent relationship with his parents, and her decision to get pregnant with their first child before he felt ready for a baby. They had six or seven good talks about these resentments. Not only did Ray forgive Susie, but also he practiced going deeper in conversation.

To stop Susie from calling family and friends to get information, Ray shared two behaviors she engaged in regularly that pushed him away. One, she got way too emotionally intense in arguments and demanded an immediate response. Two, she showed little interest in his job and did not praise him for chores he did around the home. He admitted she had lowered her emotional intensity and gave him time to process, but he told her that her praise was still very weak.

Step five

Susie took to heart chapters 12, 13, and 14 on how to be a biblical wife. She worked hard to follow Ray's leadership, build respect by speaking her mind, and develop her own life outside the home. She praised him as often as possible and spent time doing his fun activities. She even initiated sex more often. She didn't greet him at the door wearing only a smile and plastic wrap, but she did ask him for sex twice a month. At their once-a-month marriage evaluation meeting, she asked Ray to tell her—*specifically*—how she was doing as his wife.

I don't want to give you the impression things were just wonderful at this stage in the process. They weren't. But four months into the Husband Transformation Strategy, Susie was making progress. She was changing Ray and their marriage. Not major, earth-shaking change, but pretty good, steady change. Encouraging. But not enough. Although it was a safe bet that Ray would continue to improve, it was time now for my secret weapon: the Trojan horse.

Step six

I explained to Susie the importance of cleaning out her past pain with Ray's help. After going over the how-tos, I asked Susie whom she needed to write first. As her eyes filled with tears, she replied: "My dad." Here is what she wrote to the first man in her life:

> Dear Dad:
>
> I feel so strange as I sit here writing this letter to you. I don't know quite what to say, but I have so many things to say. I'm a grown woman now, but I feel like a little girl again as I reflect on what you were like as a dad and on my relationship with you.
>
> Daddy, I loved you so much when I was a child. I was a real "Daddy's girl," wasn't I? My first memory of you is sitting with you on the old green couch watching television. Just being near you was comforting for me. I can remember waiting for you to come home from work. I'd be at the window, and as soon as your car pulled into the driveway, I would run out to give you a big hug. I always had to carry your briefcase inside.

As far back as I can remember, I wanted to be close to you. Emotionally close, I mean. I wanted you and needed you to spend time with me, talk with me, play with me, be affectionate to me, and love me. Daddy, we both know those things didn't happen. I loved you desperately, but I never really felt like you loved me back. Mom always told me you loved me, but I couldn't tell. I didn't see your love. I couldn't feel it.

For years and years I've covered up my pain by telling myself: "That's just the way Dad is." Well, that is the way you have been and still are, but I have to tell you: it hurts. Your lack of expressed love angers me and hurts me deeply. It's time for me to be honest. By telling you the truth and expressing my emotions, I'll be able to clean out my pain. I'll be able to forgive you. And I'll be able to improve my marriage. Because, Dad, your mistakes and the pain you caused have transferred to Ray.

Dad, you were home just about every night and weekend. But you weren't really home because you were too busy to spend time with me. Paperwork. Paying bills. Watching television. Reading the paper. Tinkering on that stupid old, beat-up car. I wanted to talk with you and play with you, but you wouldn't do it. You always said: "Not now, honey, Dad's busy."

I'd ask you to play Barbies. You'd say no. I'd ask you to color with me in my coloring book. You'd say no. I'd ask you to swing with me on the swing set. You'd say no. I'd ask you to read to me. You'd say no. You spent more time with my brother, Dan. You played sports outside with him and watched sports on television with him. I felt rejected by you. I didn't think I was good enough, pretty enough, or smart enough to get your love and attention.

I also couldn't please you. I thought if I got good grades, obeyed you, and kept my room clean, you'd love me. But I was never good enough for you. My grades weren't all As, my room could have been cleaner, and you always pointed out my mistakes.

You didn't say, "I love you." Oh, how I longed to hear those words! I still do. You weren't very affectionate, Dad. When I turned twelve and started to develop physically, you backed off even further. Dad, you broke my heart when you did that. I needed you more in those awkward teenage years, but you weren't there for me.

Do you have any idea how painful it was to not emotionally connect with the most important man in my life? I tried everything to get you to notice me, but I failed and failed and failed. I cried myself to sleep so many nights I can't count them all.

Do you remember my tenth birthday party? I do. You had promised to take me and my two best friends to a local theme park for the day. You promised! I looked forward to that day for weeks. At the last minute you canceled because of some work thing. I was crushed. Mom ended up taking us, but it wasn't the same.

Finally I kind of gave up on you and started looking for love in other places. The wrong places. As soon as I moved into high school and boys noticed me, I started obsessing about the opposite sex. I *lived* for their attention and affection. You used to comment on how I always had a boyfriend and would spend as much time with guys as possible. Why do you think I did that, Dad?

I let guys touch me, fondle me, and even have intercourse with me. I figured it was a good trade: their love and attention for sex. It wasn't a good trade. It hurt me terribly. I accept responsibility for my actions, but I resent you for setting me up to be vulnerable and needy.

I will never forget that terrible night when you caught Johnny and me making out in the back of his car. You said: "Why do you have to be such a slut, Susie?" I can still feel the anger, shame, and humiliation. Why do you think I went too far with guys, Dad? I was searching for the love and attention that you never gave me. I know I was wrong and that my sins are my fault. But I often wonder what my dating life would have been like if you would have met my needs.

Dad, I have also resented you for years because of your lousy job as a husband. I felt so bad for Mom. Seeing you ignore her, criticize her housekeeping and appearance, and bark at her in anger, over and over. It made me so angry at you. Mom just took your abuse in stride, but I knew she was dying inside. When I complained to her about how you treated us, the two women in your life, she'd say: "That's just Daddy. He's a good man. He really doesn't mean it."

Well, Dad, those words never comforted me. Your behavior cut me deeply and shaped me as a person. I have always struggled with liking myself. Your lack of expressed love hurt my confidence. If I wasn't good enough for you to love, I thought I wasn't good enough for anyone else. I was so desperate to be loved that I moved too quickly to marry my first husband, Bernie. I thought he was a great guy and would make me happy. All he did was emotionally and physically abuse me until I finally had had enough. If you'd loved me and been the dad I needed, would I have chosen a better husband? I think so.

My stuffed resentments against you have hurt my marriage with Ray. I love Ray, and I do believe we can still have a great, close marriage. But we struggle to be close. One of the reasons is because I transfer my pain with you to him. When Ray disappoints me or hurts me, even if he does it unintentionally, I get way too upset because it reminds me of how you treated me in the past. When I lose it and start yelling and crying, Ray backs off. Then as I see any chance for understanding and intimacy slipping away, I go ballistic.

Dad, I'm writing you all this not to blame you for the mistakes I've made in my life. I'm writing to get all my anger, hurt, and resentment out. I want to purge my heart of all this pain and forgive you. I've carried it long enough.

With God's power and Ray's help I will forgive you. I want to be healthy, I want to move on, and I want to be closer to Ray. I'm reading this letter to Ray because I want him and me to work through my pain together. I'll talk about these hurtful things with Ray until I feel released and can forgive you.

I love you, and I'm going to forgive you,

Susie

The Reading

Susie set up a meeting to read Ray this letter. She asked him to listen and reflect what she said as she read. She asked him to do his best to feel her pain. Ray was visibly shaken after she finished reading. He wasn't able to do much reflecting as Susie read. He was so stunned, he couldn't get many words out of his mouth. However, he listened and did his best to comfort her. He told her he felt terrible for her and didn't realize how much pain her dad had caused. He admitted he didn't know what to say. Susie replied, "Honey, I'm just glad you listened and cared. Can you hold me for a minute?" Ray held her, and she cried for about five minutes.

Susie handed Ray the letter and asked him to read it several times before their first follow-up session. She asked him to walk in her shoes and look inside for his emotional response to her experiences, then jot down his reactions so they could discuss these at their next meeting. Wanting to help her and provide support, Ray agreed.

The Follow-Ups

Three days later, at their first follow-up meeting, Ray referred to his notes as he shared the anger he felt toward her father. The "slut" comment infuriated him. No one could say that to his woman and get away with it! Susie was gratified that Ray had, for the first time in their relationship, felt some of her pain.

In six follow-up sessions Susie vented more pain about her dad as she gradually moved from rage to hurt to deep sadness. By making herself vulnerable to Ray, she invited him inside her emotional world. Without even knowing what he was doing, Ray joined her. As he worked to understand and help her past the pain, Ray opened up emotionally.

Ray felt her pain first and then began to feel some of his own. Thinking about his own father, he realized their two dads exhibited similar behavior. He felt anger at his rigid, unemotional, unaffectionate father and shared this with Susie. She listened, reflected, and thanked him for opening up about it. She didn't ask him to do more work on his dad. Yet.

By the fourth follow-up meeting it dawned on Ray that he was like Susie's father. He hated that realization but told Susie that he could no longer deny it. He could see how his IA behavior reminded her of her dad and triggered her pain. He finally understood Susie's intense reactions when he failed to meet her emotional and spiritual needs.

Of course the follow-ups weren't all filled with good emotional connections and intimate, healing moments. Many times Ray made communication mistakes. He got logical or overwhelmed by her intense pain and lost track of what she was saying. Sometimes he grew silent and gave no response. Other times he got impatient and irritable because he couldn't fix the situation. Each time he veered off track, Susie called him on it. After a five- or ten-minute break, they resumed the meeting.

During one of the early follow-ups Susie blew up when Ray told her he thought she was being too hard on her father. She told him she needed a break and would come to him when she was ready to continue. After twenty minutes she restarted the meeting and told Ray that his comment had angered and hurt her. She needed listening and understanding, not editorial comments supporting her father. Ray apologized and returned to understanding mode.

Ray did a decent job of communicating with Susie during these follow-ups. Although he made mistakes, he learned from them. His summary letter showed Susie that he had been listening and gained some valuable insights into her and their marriage. Susie thanked Ray over and over again for his willingness to talk with her about her dad, for his effort, and for his supportive, emotionally connecting statements.

While these conversations were designed to help Susie, they also helped Ray by bringing him to a deeper emotional level with Susie. Gradually he became more comfortable with that. Instead of loathing intimacy and avoiding a deeper level of conversation, he at first tolerated it and then developed an appreciation for its benefits.

More Letters

Susie wrote two more letters: one to her abusive, dirt-ball ex-husband and one to the baby she aborted. These letters were even more painful and heart-wrenching than the one to her dad. As she experienced healing from these traumatic experiences, Ray learned more about understanding and connecting with his wife. When she read her letter to her dead baby, they both shed tears. Ray had known about the abortion before their marriage, but he hadn't known what Susie endured before, during, and after the procedure.

Ray listened, reflected, supported, and encouraged. By feeling her pain as best he could, Ray did what no man had ever done for Susie before. Ray did what *he* had never done before. He connected with Susie on a deep, personal, intimate level. Through this he realized what he had been missing his whole marriage. The work wasn't over; the work of marriage is never over. Yet it had certainly begun.

It's Your Turn, Baby

When Susie finished her letters and all the follow-up meetings, she called another. By now Ray was so used to them that he didn't even flinch. At this meeting Susie asked him to heal from *his* past pain with her help. She asked him to do what she had just done: write letters and do follow-up meetings. She said she wanted to help him heal the way she had—and that she wanted to get even closer to him in their relationship. She gave him two weeks to think and pray about it.

After a few weeks of waffling, Ray agreed. He had already admitted pain with his dad, so he couldn't very well deny he had issues in his past. He ended up writing letters to his dad, his mom, and an ex-fiancée. Through his readings and follow-up discussions, they grew even closer.

What If He Says No?

If your husband balks at identifying and working on his past pain, take these four steps:

1. Call another meeting and ask him to take a week and jot down all his reasons for not doing this project. After a week meet again and discuss his reasons. Come up with a list of reasons why you think he is resisting and discuss these with him. You may be able to talk him through his reluctance.

2. Call another meeting. At that meeting ask him to write down a list of persons who have caused him significant pain in the past. Give him two weeks to complete his list. Then tell him if he can't come up with one, you will do some research—namely, call his family and friends—and develop a list for him. Your offer to "help" may spur him on to put his list together.

3. At the next meeting ask what he discovered. If he has a list, you ask him again to write letters and schedule follow-up meetings. If he has no list or has one but refuses to write to these individuals, tell him you love him too much to drop the issue. Inform him you're going to work as an HPI: Husband's Pain Investigator. You will make calls, send e-mails, do lunches, and gather data on his past pain and the sources. Having lived with the man and because you know his family, you already have a head start.

4. When you have gathered all the information on the pain-causers and what they did to him, call another meeting. You read to him what you have learned, laying out in front of him the pain from his past. Ask him again to follow the same healing steps you followed. Make it clear it is up to him and you will wait for him to tell you he is ready. As you wait, use one-way communication to show him how past pain transfers to the present:

- "You clammed up, just like when your mom hurt you. Until you deal with her, you'll keep shutting me out."

- "There you go again, not trusting me. Your ex-wife burned you badly, and until you clean out your pain with her, you'll never trust me."

- "I just tried to get close to you and you picked a fight and raised your voice. That's just like your dad. It's a pattern you won't break until you write him an honest letter and we talk about your pain with him."

Remember to avoid meanness or sarcasm with these comments. You need to simply tell him the truth in a brief, honest, straightforward manner.

Let's Do It Again...and Again

With gentle guidance from me, Ray and Susie discovered that they could follow the same basic six-step process when dealing with any other major issue in their relationship. Whether it was a personal issue or some kind of a conflict, they followed the same steps.

One of them would call a meeting. At that session the spouse with the issue would make an opening statement. Sometimes the speaking spouse would read a letter detailing facts, thoughts, and emotions. The other spouse wouldn't say anything original, just listen and reflect. The listening spouse's job was to build understanding and walk in the other spouse's shoes.

Once the speaking spouse felt genuinely understood, the meeting ended. But not before they scheduled a follow-up discussion. This second meeting might take place a day or two later, and be as short as ten minutes. At the second meeting the spouse who had listened now became the speaker and shared his/her reactions and view of the issue. Now the other spouse needed to be heard and understood.

Ray and Susie would have as many follow-up meetings as necessary to work through the issue. Since they had practiced this process with very painful, difficult issues as they healed from the past, they had the steps down cold. They could now follow the same steps with current-day issues, most of which were not nearly as intense as their past pain. They knew how to work together, communicate, and connect. The same can be true of your marriage.

STEP SEVEN

I NEED TO GET TOUGH AND RATTLE YOUR CAGE

Chapter 17

If He Stays Clammed Up, It's Time to Confront

Y OU HAVE TAKEN all the steps in my Husband Transformation Strategy. You have created a team. Asked your husband to read the chapters on being a biblical husband. Written a letter to him communicating your needs. Forgiven him for his past mistakes. Continued to keep your system clean of resentments by using one-way communication. Addressed your half of your marital problems and worked hard to be a biblical wife. Healed from your past pain and included your husband in the process.

And your husband is still an intimacy avoider. He hasn't changed. Sure, he went through these six steps with you, but his heart wasn't in it. It was obvious his heart wasn't in it. Or he may have done a few steps with you before quitting. Or steadfastly refused to do any of them. He is among the 10 percent of intimacy avoiders who do not respond to steps one through six. He has dug in his heels, refusing to open up to you and meet your needs. *You* are stronger and healthier as a person, but *he's* pretty much the same old IA, leaving you no closer to a personal, intimate marriage.

Ignore the "Experts"

What do you do now? If you turn to the leading Christian "experts" on marriage, they will tell you there isn't much you can—or should—do. In fact, they would be horrified to know you have already taken the action steps described in this book. These recognized Christian authorities will tell you to just continue pursuing your husband while being patient and acting as a good, dutiful wife: "Smile, honey, and keep on meeting his needs, regardless of his behavior. Just submit and pray for him."

This extremely popular advice from well-meaning Christian leaders is wrong. Wrong. Wrong. Wrong. Dead wrong, and it will not work. It will ruin you emotionally, physically, and spiritually. And it will enable your husband to stay an intimacy avoider. Most of all it is not what the Bible says to do.

Listen to the Bible

The Bible says your husband is a sinner. When he knows what your needs are and still refuses to meet them, he is a sinner. When you have clearly described how his actions have hurt you and he continues, he is a sinner. When he doesn't respond to you speaking the truth in love about his behavior, he is a sinner. When you have done everything you can do to be a biblical wife and he couldn't care less, he is a sinner. When you risked vulnerability by being open about your past pain and he is unmoved, he is a sinner.

He is sinning in an intentional, willful way. He has not repented or changed, even though he now knows what God wants him to do as your husband. With his eyes wide open he is breaking God's laws concerning his role as a husband (Eph. 5:25–33; 1 Pet. 3:7; Col. 3:19). He has moved from merely acting as an intimacy avoider to a husband who is actively sinning.

Although I have mentioned this passage previously, it is a good time to remind you what the Bible says to do with someone involved in serious sin:

> If your brother sins, go and show him his fault in private; if
> he listens to you, you have won your brother. But if he does

not listen to you, take one or two more with you, so that by the mouth of two or three witnesses every fact may be confirmed. If he refuses to listen to them, tell it to the church; and if he refuses to listen even to the church, let him be to you as a Gentile and a tax collector.

—MATTHEW 18:15–17

This is the same passage I quoted in chapter 13 when I addressed the abusive husband. Guess what? Your husband has advanced to the abuser category. He is not only trashing the sacred institution of marriage, but he is also emotionally abusing you and, indirectly, the children. God wants you to confront your abusive, sinning husband the Matthew 18 way.

My purpose in this chapter is not to set forth a detailed Matthew Confrontation Plan. I wrote an entire book about how to confront a sinning husband (*What to Do When Your Spouse Says, I Don't Love You Anymore*). If you are in this situation after step six of my Husband Transformation Strategy, get that book. Here I will give you a brief overview of what you have to do. Keep in mind that these biblical actions are a last resort.

Confront Him Three Times

Gather your support team. Tell them where you are in the process and what you plan to do now. Read Matthew 18:15–17 aloud and pray together that God will use these steps to break your husband and cause him to genuinely confess and repent. Ask your team to pray during each of your coming confrontations.

Go to your husband to schedule a meeting. Make sure the kids are out of the house when the meeting takes place. At the meeting tell him he has clearly chosen to not be the husband you need and the husband God commands him to be. Inform him that his choice and continuing mistreatment of you makes him a sinner. Tell him you are going to follow the Bible and confront his sin. Then read Matthew 18:15–17.

Tell him he already knows what you need. Inform him that you are giving him one week to think and pray about his sin. Make it clear that if he acknowledges his sin and proves to you a heartfelt desire to repent—that is, change—you won't take any of the other Matthew 18 steps. However, if he chooses not to repent, you will go to the next step.

If he shows no signs of repentance after a week, summon one or two of your closest friends/family members/supporters to join you in confronting him again. Do not stall. Move with speed. You have waited long enough for the man to change. Do not give your husband any warning. This is a surprise attack. Just show up. Ideally one of these "witnesses" needs to be a man who knows your husband well. Let this man or another member of your intervention group do the talking. They should deliver the same message: "You are sinning. You need to repent and take action to genuinely change as a husband. You have one week to show your wife and us that you are serious about changing."

If, after seven more days, he remains unmoved, go to your pastor and church leaders. Take your team members/witnesses with you. Explain in detail the pitiful state of your marriage, the steps you have taken trying to change it, and how your husband is sinning against you and God. Tell these leaders you have moved through the first two confrontations required by Matthew 18. Urge them to form a team to quickly intervene with your husband. Give them three weeks to take action. If your church leaders fail to follow through, don't be shocked. Many pastors and church leaders will not agree with the assertive, tough love action you are demanding. They are more likely to just ask you to be patient and submissive. They will probably tell you that if you just love him enough, he will change. They may even blame your marriage problems on you or ask what you have done to create such a crisis.

Don't hold your breath waiting for them to confront your husband. In addition to many church leaders failing to agree with my approach, it is highly likely they don't have the guts to confront your husband. Confrontation is tough, and many church leaders avoid doing it. There are some who will confront sinners and enforce church discipline, but there aren't many. If your church leaders refuse to confront your husband and blame you for your husband's behavior, it's going to hurt you. Really hurt you. And yet, I want you to ask for their help because it's what the Bible instructs you to do. You've taken many healthy steps in my strategy at this point, and I think you're ready to deal with this kind of rejection. Just be prepared for a very negative, disappointing reaction, and if that's what happens, do three things. One, rely on God for His strength and comfort. Two, lean on your support team. Three, find a new church where the leaders follow the Bible. Then move on to the next step in God's plan.

Shun Him

By now if your husband has weathered three interventions (or two, if your pastor and his team have "choked" and done nothing) and clearly isn't about to budge, your job is to shake him as he has never been shaken before. You have reached the end of the Matthew 18 process. Without further discussion you must immediately "let him be to you as a Gentile and a tax collector" (v. 17). I didn't say divorce him. I never recommend divorce. You will first shun him. If that doesn't break him, you should physically separate.

As you start this shunning, gather your children and tell them exactly what you are doing and why. Tell them Daddy is sinning by treating you badly. Give them appropriate, specific examples of his mistreatment. Explain what you have done to try and change him. Read the Matthew 18 passage and describe the interventions you instigated to obey God's Word. Let them know that you are shunning Dad in an attempt to force true repentance.

223

Be clear that if their father doesn't respond to this, you will take steps to separate from him.

Shunning means that for one full month you ignore your husband. You act as if he doesn't exist and talk to him only when absolutely necessary (such as an emergency situation). Move out of the bedroom. Provide no services to him of any kind. No communication. No "good morning" greetings. No time together. No food preparation for him. No laundry for him. No sex. You don't sit with him in church. You don't sit with him at your children's school and sporting events. He doesn't exist.

If he is stupid enough to ask why, you ignore him. He knows why. You are obeying the Bible and creating a crisis in his life. He needs to see that he has lost you. You *have had it.* You are over him and his sin. Will he miss you? Will he want you back? You will see. A stubborn, prideful, sinful husband will change only when he realizes he has lost his wife.

If after this month of shunning he remains in sin, make preparations to physically separate. Again remind your children of what you are doing and why. Break your silence by asking him to leave the home. If he refuses or is obviously stalling, take the children and leave. (However, if you can't afford to move out or have no place to go, remain at home and stay in the shunning mode.)

If at any point in the Matthew 18 confrontation process he shows signs of breaking and repentance, be wary. Stay pulled back and do not just jump back into his arms. Talk is cheap. So are empty promises. Require action. If he says he is ready to change, hand him a list of what he needs to do.

See a Christian psychologist/therapist of *your* choosing.

You should attend the first session so you can assure he provides the counselor the true picture, not a smokescreen of self-justification or blame-shifting. Insist that your husband go to two months of individual therapy and work on his blocks to intimacy.

Require him to sign a confidentiality release form that allows the therapist to offer you regular updates on his progress.

Meet with your pastor.

As with his therapist, you should attend the first meeting. The purpose is to develop a spiritual growth program that he will follow for at least two months. It will include regular church attendance, a small group Bible study, a men's support group (such as Celebrate Recovery), and one-on-one discipleship. He must continue the support group and discipleship relationship for at least one year.

Find an older, godly man to serve as his accountability partner.

This could be the same guy who is discipling him. They will meet face-to-face weekly, except in unusual situations, such as out-of-town travel or illness. He will have an accountability partner for the rest of his life

He will work to be the best husband he can be for two months.

He will read chapters 5, 6, and 7 and be that kind of husband. In fact, recommend that he read the whole book and make you believe he is willing to follow my advice.

If he follows through on these behaviors and shows progress after two months, only then should you respond favorably and agree to enter marriage counseling. Under the guidance of your therapist, you will go back through my Husband Transformation Strategy. This time require that he dedicate himself to following these steps with energy and passion.

While I hope and pray that you don't have to carry out step seven of my strategy, this may be necessary. In any case, don't hesitate. Gather your support team and, with Jesus at your side, do it.

"How Long Do I Wait for Him to Change?"

This is an excellent, practical question. The answer: only God knows. I never recommend divorce—never have and never will. That is not my business. Ending a marriage is *always* God's business. I get angry whenever I hear that anyone in a helping role, whether a pastor, therapist, author, family member, or friend, has recommended a divorce. Seek God's guidance, and He *will* show you what He wants you to do.

Your sinning husband may divorce you. God may release you from your marriage and allow you to divorce your husband. God may reveal to you that He wants you to stay in your lonely, painful marriage with a sinful spouse—at least, for now. If you believe God wants you to stay, I wrote chapter 18 for you.

PART THREE
WHAT IF GOD WANTS ME TO STAY IN A LONELY MARRIAGE?

Chapter 18

Living With a Man
Who Won't Change

Y OU HAVE DONE all you can to try to bring about change in your husband. You went through the first six steps of my Husband Transformation Strategy, but he is still the same old husband. Then you applied step seven, the Matthew 18 tough love approach. He is still the same old husband. In fact, he is a bit more difficult to live with. Were you to stand today before God, you could assure Him that you have done your absolute best to create a different husband and a different marriage.

Though your husband has chosen to remain just the way he is, you believe God wants you to stay married to him. Maybe you're convinced it's best for your children. You don't want your precious children to suffer the damage of divorce. I don't blame you.

So you're staying with him. About now you may also be asking yourself, "How do I stay with a man like this? How do I avoid being a doormat who is chronically depressed and miserable? How can I continue to be an assertive, strong, and healthy woman?" Here is how.*

Believe He Is Never Going to Change

Give up all hope that he is going to change. He had his chance and stubbornly refuses to budge a quarter inch. Until he draws

---

* Many of the strategies in this chapter were contributed by my therapy associate, Laurel A. Slade, MS.

his last breath, he is staying exactly the same husband he is right now. The brutal truth is he doesn't love you. He has feelings for you, but he is incapable of loving you. He is incapable of loving anyone but himself. My associate, Laurel Slade, says: "You have to radically accept that you are married to a narcissist." He is not merely selfish; he is super-selfish. World-class selfish. Everything he thinks, feels, and does focuses on one goal: to protect and please himself.

Check out this profile of a narcissist:

- He has no empathy.

- He has no capacity for compassion.

- He cannot care for anyone but himself.

- He will not meet your needs; your needs don't even register on his radar screen.

- When he does something nice for you, it is for the purpose of getting something from you.

- It is always and forever about him. It is never about you.

- Nothing is ever his fault; it is always someone else's fault.

- Perfect persons don't make mistakes, and he believes he's perfect.

- The very idea of his changing is ludicrous to him, because one doesn't need to change when one is perfect.

- He intensely rejects any criticism, because he cannot allow his vision of personal perfection to be tarnished in the slightest way.

- However, he is very critical of you: your weight, your cooking, your housekeeping, your parenting, or your serving at church (because it detracts from serving him).

- He is always the smartest and best-looking person in the room.

- He is convinced that you should spend every waking minute being unbelievably grateful that he married you.

- He manipulates everyone to get his way.

- He makes decisions without consulting you.

- He is condescending, because he believes he is better than anyone else.

- Using sarcasm often, he thinks he is being "funny," but his comments hurt you.

- He is a bully who intimidates others.

- He can be charming and charismatic in social environments.

- He loves money and spends it the way he wants to spend it.

- Every decision he makes is based on what will make him look good, what will make him happy, and what is best for him.

- He lies often. What's worse, he believes his own lies.

- He lives in a universe of one: I want. I need. I desire. I, I, I, I.

- He believes all others exist to serve him and meet his needs.

Recognize your husband in this profile? I'll bet you do. He is not evil or intentionally malicious. He is just incredibly—and permanently—focused on himself. In his world it is all about him. Unless he fully surrenders to God, it always will be. However, in the brave new world where I want you to venture, it will not be about him anymore. It is about God, you, and your children.

Of course you and your children will continue to pray for this man who is your husband and their father. But you are through hoping that he will change and trying to change him. You're through trying to figure out why he is the way he is. That is over with now. You don't take any of the steps in this chapter to change him. Instead, follow them to build and nourish your physical, psychological, and spiritual health, and that of your children.

Require Three Bottom-Line Behaviors

That last section is pretty depressing, isn't it? Still, it is reality. He is a narcissist, and he is not going to change. However, if he wants to continue living with you, you must demand three "bottom-line" behaviors. These will not produce any change in him, but they will provide essential protection and security for you and your children. Living with a narcissist is one thing; living with an out-of-control, abusive narcissist is quite another. While you can do the first (that is, live with him), you must not allow the second.

Be crystal clear that as long as he continues the behaviors I am going to outline shortly, you will live with him. (At least, you will unless God directs you to separate from him.) If he chooses to not do all of these behaviors, you will work with an attorney about separation arrangements. When you give him this ultimatum, you can't be bluffing. He will know you don't mean it. You must be serious and willing to bring down the hammer. If you cannot afford to physically separate, create a separate home: separate bedrooms and the shunning I described in chapter 17.

Except this time the shunning continues indefinitely. You will communicate with him only when necessary.

If you physically separate, or separate at home, tell your children the truth: "I am setting strict boundaries with your father. These boundaries include separation, just as God separated from the Israelites when their hearts were hard." This reinforces that God's direction is being followed. Explain each behavior to them and tell them the truth—that if you separate physically, "Failing to do this will severely damage all of us—physically, emotionally, and spiritually."

If he decides to follow the behaviors, require that he do them, initially, for one month. If he complies with a decent attitude, then you may end the separation.

The first behavior is *complete openness and honesty*. This means he must provide you with access to his cell phone and all computer accounts, including passwords. He cannot object to you reviewing his text messages, e-mails, or Facebook posts. Realistically you can't trust him, so you need to know if he is engaging in any kind of behavior that will harm you or the kids. Most narcissists will whine, "OK, I want access to your stuff too!" Your response: "Fine. I don't have anything to hide."

Second: require *a daily devotional and prayer time together*, twenty to thirty minutes in length. This gives you a spiritual connection and a daily opportunity for God to work on him.

The third behavior is *regular attendance at a couples small group*. This will be with couples from your church or a similar group. It will provide good teaching on marriage and relationships and friendships with other couples, while exerting social pressure on your husband to be a decent husband.

Again these bottom-line behaviors will not change your husband. However, they will restrain him from damaging or destructive actions that may jeopardize the safety and security and well-being of you and your children. The next four steps in my Living With a Man Who Won't Change Game Plan come from previous chapters. I will briefly summarize these steps and identify the chapters where they are located. You may want to reread them as a refresher course on these self-care areas.

1. Team up (chapter 3).

To live successfully with a narcissist, you need a close and growing relationship with Jesus Christ. A thirty- to forty-five minute quiet time with Jesus *every day* is vital. You need God's power and protection, because your husband may likely do things that hurt you every day. Also, rounding out your team should be a best friend of the same sex, a small group of diehard supporters, and a caring church.

2. Forgive him, and keep on forgiving him (chapters 8–10).

To get rid of bitterness and resentment, you must forgive him for all he has done in the past to hurt you. Use the one-way communication technique to keep your system clean of resentments. With your narcissist, don't use one-way communication to try to change his mind, but to maintain your assertiveness, strength, and health.

3. Take care of yourself, because no one else will (chapter 12).

If you plan to not just survive but live a quality life, you must get regular mental health breaks from your husband and children. If your selfish husband refuses to watch the kids for these personal getaways, ask a family member, friend, or babysitter. Assume he is irresponsible and turn to him last (not first) to take care of the kids. Develop an interesting, need-meeting life by building friendships, serving in your church, enjoying a hobby, and doing volunteer work. You might continue your education or find a rewarding job outside the home.

4. Offer conditional submission (chapter 13).

Do not submit in any way to an abusive husband. If he is abusing you, physically or emotionally, take aggressive action—and take it quickly. Tell your support team the truth, and follow the tough love steps from Matthew 18:15–17.

Since he is an active and ongoing, serious sinner, do not submit to him in the fullest sense of that biblical term. If his decisions are reasonable and in accord with the Bible, support him. But if his decisions prove selfish and anti-biblical, do not support him. He will be furious, but that's just too bad. Ultimately you submit to God and His principles.

Because it is highly likely that Mr. Narcissist won't act as the spiritual leader of your family, you will have to assume those duties. You will lead family devotions at least once a week and each week make sure the kids get to church, Sunday school classes, and weekly age-appropriate youth group activities.

Praise the Positives

Even with a narcissist a behavior rewarded is a behavior repeated. While your praise won't change who he is, it can motivate him to do good things. He will tend to continue behaviors for which he gets praised. Such praise will make him feel good about himself—his number-one priority in life.

Be Honest With the Kids

When your husband mistreats you in front of the children, immediately and assertively correct him—in front of them. This firm response will maintain their respect for you and decrease this disrespectful behavior. Later in private explain to each child how Dad's behavior was wrong and hurtful. Be careful not to degrade him or speak in a deliberately unkind manner; just tell the truth. Also, teach each child the proper and biblical way to treat a person. Again and again your message to your children will be: Dad is wrong, the Bible is right.

If he mistreats the kids in your presence, quickly step in to protect them. This will limit the damage and show them that "you have their back" when Dad is mean. Later in private explain how Dad was wrong and the Bible is right. Always encourage your children to talk with you about their father and express openly the way they feel about his hurtful, selfish behavior.

Let them know this is about them, not about changing their dad. It is a good idea to take them to a Christian counselor to learn coping skills and how to guard their hearts (Prov. 4:23). As they get older, they will develop a better understanding of his narcissism. Despite recognizing he is a narcissist, they can still love him while learning to become others-centered followers of Jesus Christ.

Be Careful With Other Men

Because your narcissistic husband won't meet your needs, you are incredibly vulnerable to other men. You can easily find yourself drawn to another man who gives you attention and appears to be *so different* from your husband in so many important ways. Guard against this by maintaining firm boundaries with both single and married men. Do not have private, personal talks with any man other than your husband. Build deep relationships with women, and get your needs met from the healthy sources I described in chapter 13. Get an accountability partner, and have her watch your relationships with men very closely.

Be Joan of Arc not
Joan of Codependency

You can live with a narcissist and still be a healthy woman with a good life. You can live with a narcissist and raise healthy, successful, Christ-following children. To do it, you must be tough, honest, and assertive. If you give in to weakness and stuff your feelings while passively allowing him to mistreat you, then you and your kids will suffer serious damage. I am not exaggerating. I have seen far too many wives and children harmed in terrible, long-lasting ways by narcissistic men. Don't go down that road. If you need help to follow my strategy, see a Christian therapist.

With God's help and hard work, you really can be Joan of Arc (with the exception of the whole burned-at-the-stake thing). You can be courageous. You and your kids can live God's adventure for your lives. So as God told Joshua:

> Be strong and courageous! Do not tremble or be dismayed, for the LORD your God is with you wherever you go.
> —JOSHUA 1:9

Resources

Other Books by David Clarke

- *Men Are Clams, Women Are Crowbars: Understand Your Differences and Make Them Work*
- *A Marriage After God's Own Heart* (achieving the ultimate: spiritual intimacy in your marriage)
- *What to Do When Your Spouse Says, I Don't Love You Anymore: An Action Plan to Regain Confidence, Power, and Control* (dealing with a spouse in serious sin)
- *Parenting Isn't for Superheroes: Everyday Strategies for Raising Good Kids*
- *The Total Marriage Makeover: A Proven Plan to Revolutionize Your Marriage*
- *The 6 Steps to Emotional Freedom: Breaking Through to the Life God Wants You to Live*
- *Cinderella Meets the Caveman: Stop the Boredom in Your Marriage and Jump-Start the Passion*
- *Kiss Me Like You Mean It: Solomon's Crazy in Love How-To Manual*
- *I Don't Want a Divorce: A 90-Day Guide to Saving Your Marriage*

To schedule a seminar, order Dr. Clarke's books, set up an in-person or phone advice session, and access his speaking schedule, please contact:

David Clarke Seminars
Marriage & Family Enrichment Center
6505 North Himes Avenue
Tampa, FL 33614
www.davidclarkeseminars.com
1-888-516-8844

About the Authors

DAVID E. CLARKE, PHD, is a Christian psychologist, speaker, and the author of nine books, including *Kiss Me Like You Mean It*. A graduate of Dallas Theological Seminary and Western Conservative Baptist Seminary in Portland, Oregon, he has been in private practice for twenty-five years. He lives in Florida with his wife, Sandy, and their four children.

WILLIAM G. CLARKE has been a marriage and family therapist for more than thirty years. He is a graduate of the University of Southern California and the California Family Study Center, where he earned his master's degree. Along with his wife, he served with Campus Crusade for Christ for nine years. He is the founder of the Marriage and Family Enrichment Center in Tampa, Florida. He lives in Tampa with his wife, Kathleen.

A Healthy Life—
body, mind, and spirit—
IS PART OF GOD'S PURPOSE FOR YOU!

Siloam brings you books, e-books, and other media from trusted authors on today's most important health topics. Check out the following links for more books from specialists such as *New York Times* best-selling author Dr. Don Colbert and get on the road to great health.

SILOAM

FREE NEWSLETTERS
TO HELP EMPOWER YOUR LIFE

Why subscribe today?

❑ **DELIVERED DIRECTLY TO YOU.** All you have to do is open your inbox and read.

❑ **EXCLUSIVE CONTENT.** We cover the news overlooked by the mainstream press.

❑ **STAY CURRENT.** Find the latest court rulings, revivals, and cultural trends.

❑ **UPDATE OTHERS.** Easy to forward to friends and family with the click of your mouse.

CHOOSE THE E-NEWSLETTER THAT INTERESTS YOU MOST:

- Christian news
- Daily devotionals
- Spiritual empowerment
- And much, much more

SIGN UP AT: **http://freenewsletters.charismamag.com**